MAX AXIOM
AND THE SOCIETY OF SUPER SCIENTISTS

THE WORLD OF
ARTIFICIAL INTELLIGENCE

BY **CAROL KIM**

ILLUSTRATED BY **ERIK DOESCHER**

CAPSTONE PRESS
a capstone imprint

Published by Capstone Press, an imprint of Capstone
1710 Roe Crest Drive
North Mankato, Minnesota 56003
capstonepub.com

Library of Congress Cataloging-in-Publication Data
is available on the Library of Congress website.
ISBN: 9781669017455 (hardcover)
ISBN: 9781669017400 (paperback)
ISBN: 9781669017417 (eBook PDF)

Summary: Computers are found everywhere in our world, and they're becoming smarter every day. But what makes a computer program intelligent? Can computers and robots really think and learn on their own? Or are they just following complex programming? Follow along with Max Axiom and the Society of Super Scientists as they learn how artificial intelligence works and how AI is used in the world today.

Editorial Credits
Editor: Aaron Sautter; Designer: Elyse White
Media Researcher: Rebekah Hubstenberger;
Production Specialist: Whitney Schaefer

All internet sites appearing in back matter were available and accurate when this book was sent to press.

Printed and bound in the USA.

TABLE OF CONTENTS

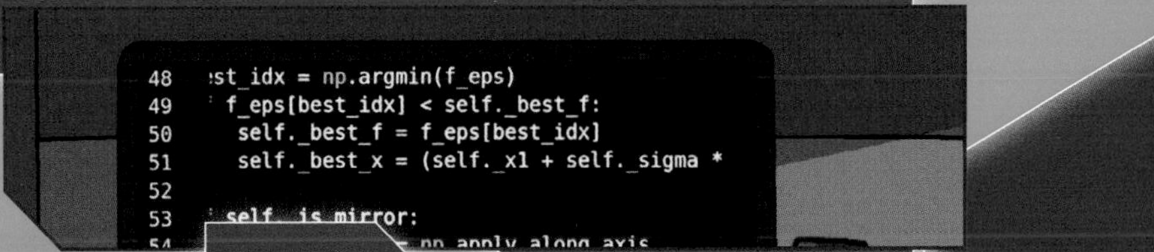

48 st_idx = np.argmin(f_eps)
49 f_eps[best_idx] < self._best_f:
50 self._best_f = f_eps[best_idx]
51 self._best_x = (self._x1 + self._sigma *
52
53 self._is_mirror:

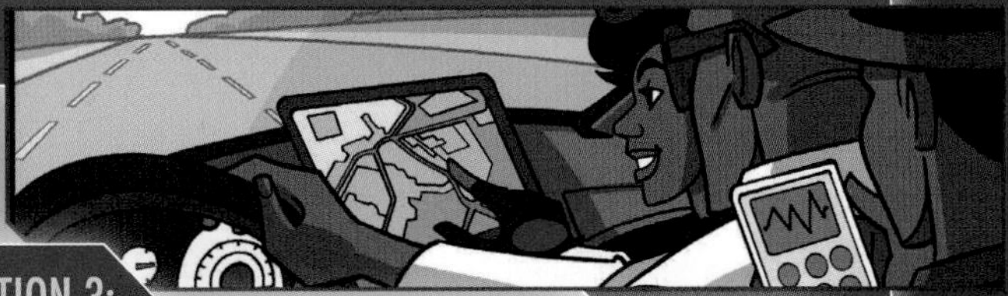

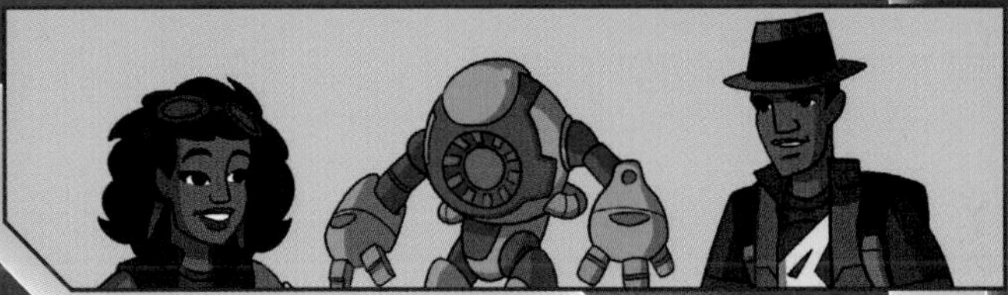

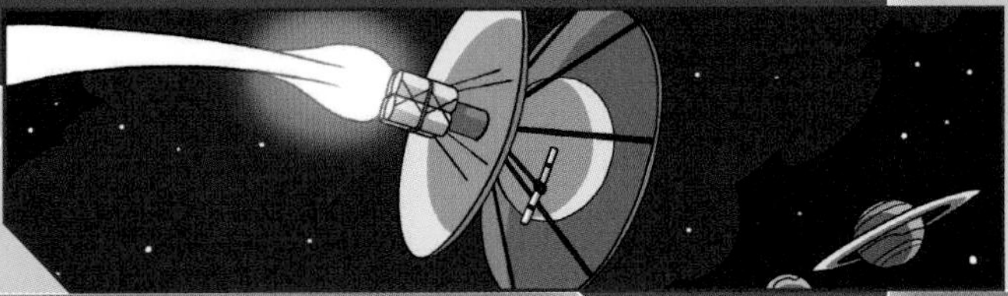

THE SOCIETY OF SUPER SCIENTISTS

MAX AXIOM

After years of study, Max Axiom, the world's first Super Scientist, knew the mysteries of the universe were too vast for one person alone to uncover. So Max created the Society of Super Scientists! Using their superpowers and super-smarts, this talented group investigates today's most urgent scientific and environmental issues and learns about actions everyone can take to solve them.

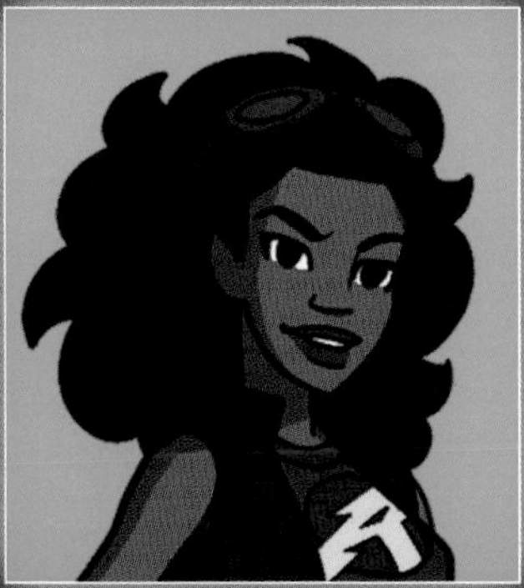

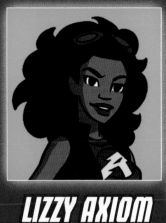

LIZZY AXIOM

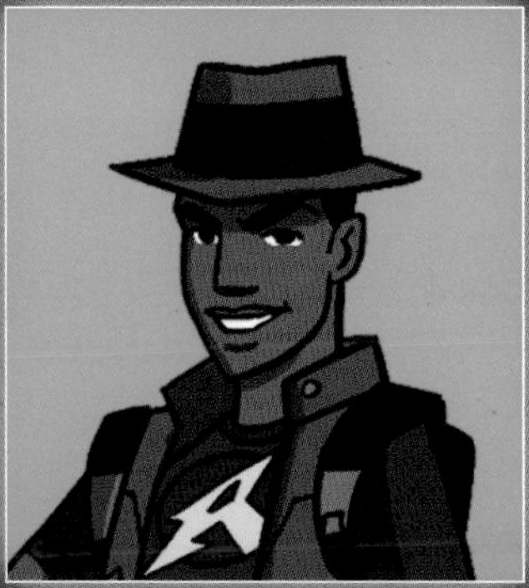

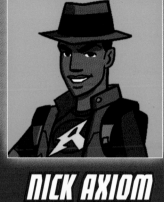

NICK AXIOM

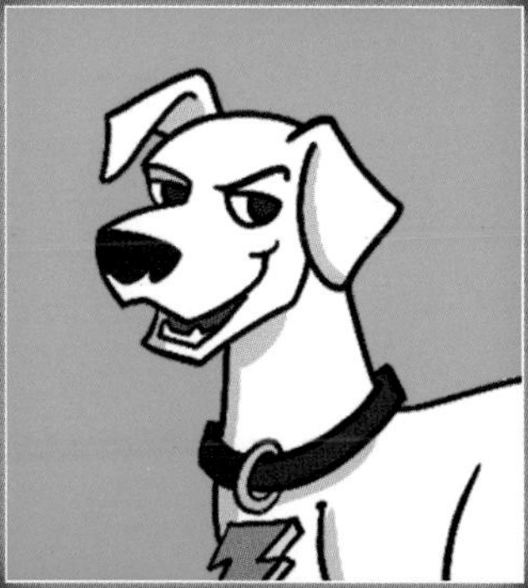

SPARK

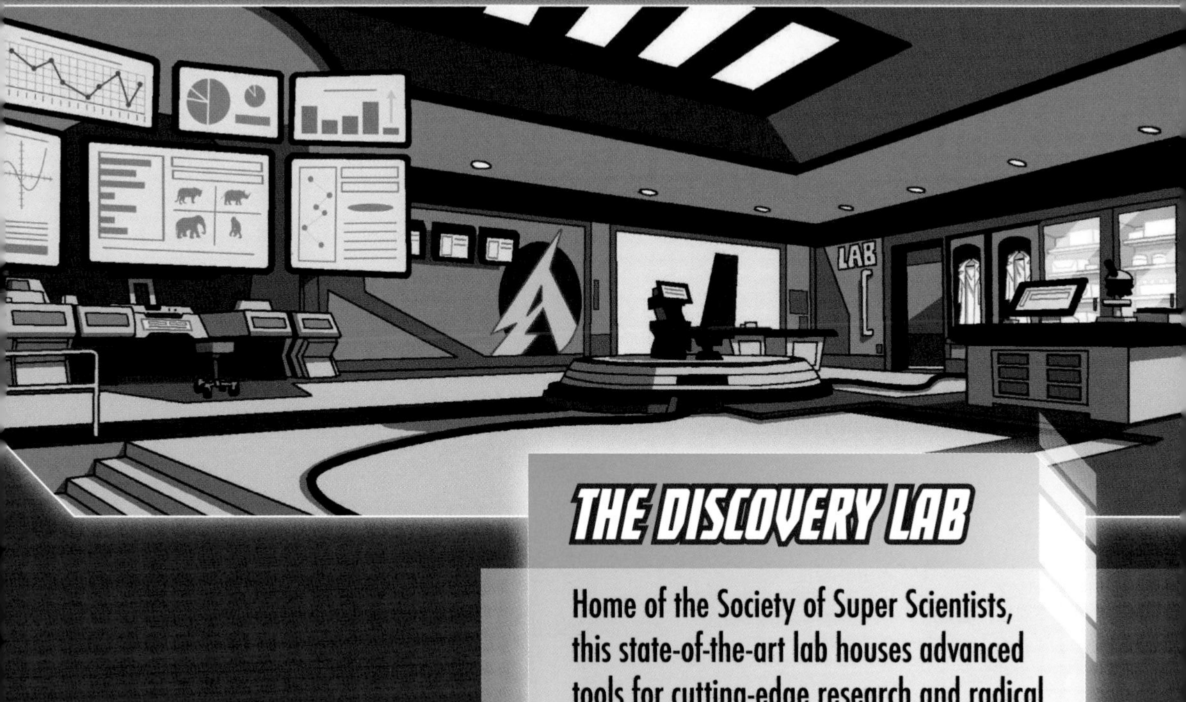
LAB

THE DISCOVERY LAB

Home of the Society of Super Scientists, this state-of-the-art lab houses advanced tools for cutting-edge research and radical scientific innovation. More importantly, it is a space for Super Scientists to collaborate and share knowledge as they work together to tackle any challenge.

SECTION 1: *WHAT IS ARTIFICIAL INTELLIGENCE?*

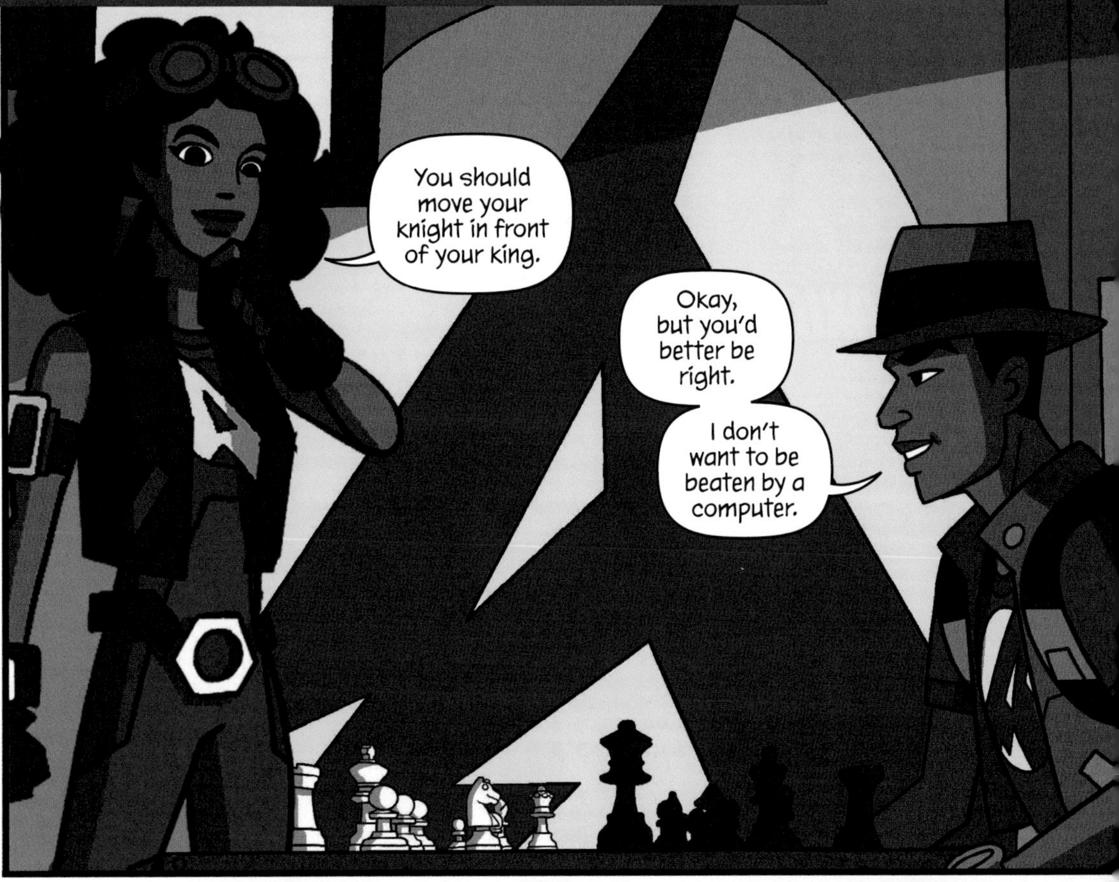

You should move your knight in front of your king.
Okay, but you'd better be right.
I don't want to be beaten by a computer.

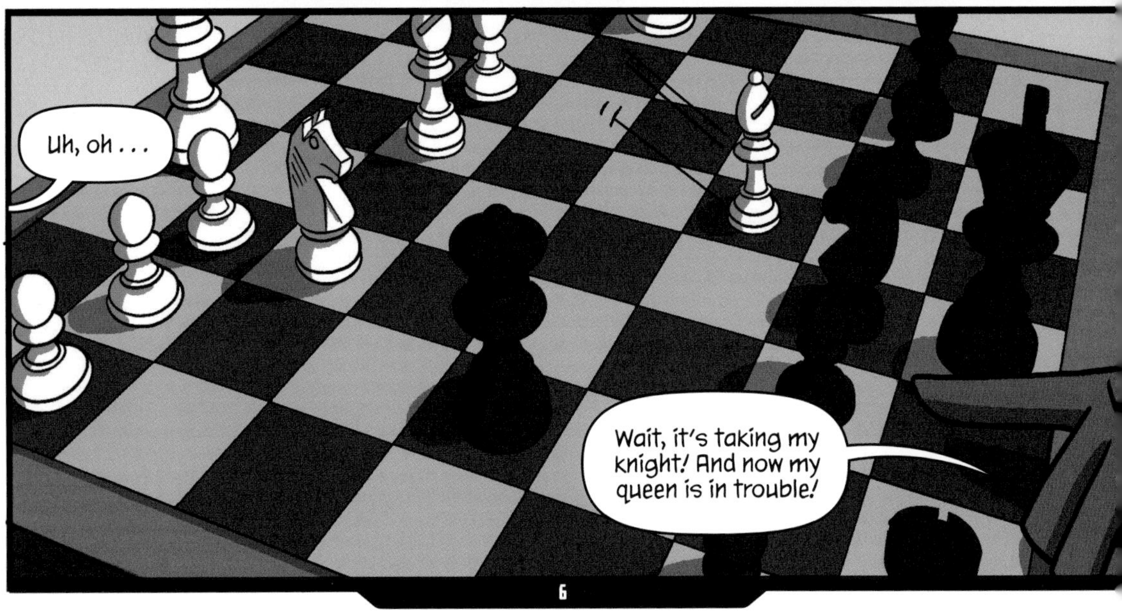

Uh, oh . . .
Wait, it's taking my knight! And now my queen is in trouble!

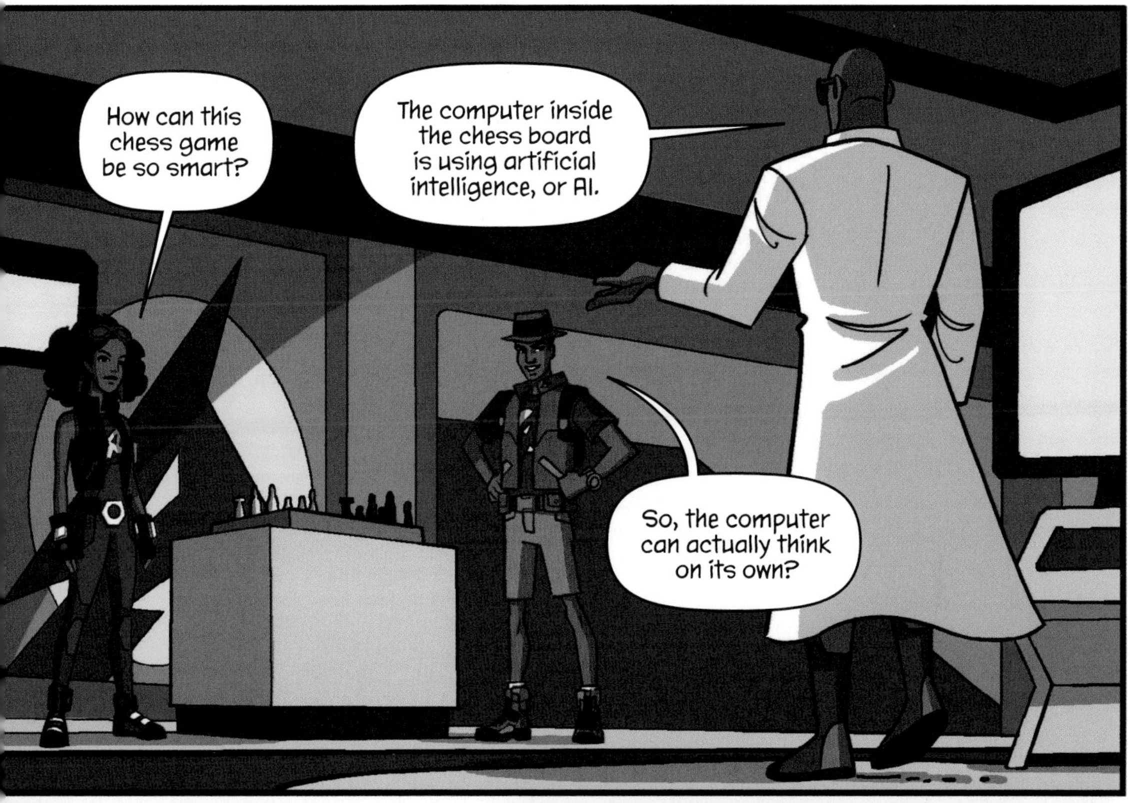
How can this chess game be so smart?
The computer inside the chess board is using artificial intelligence, or AI.
So, the computer can actually think on its own?

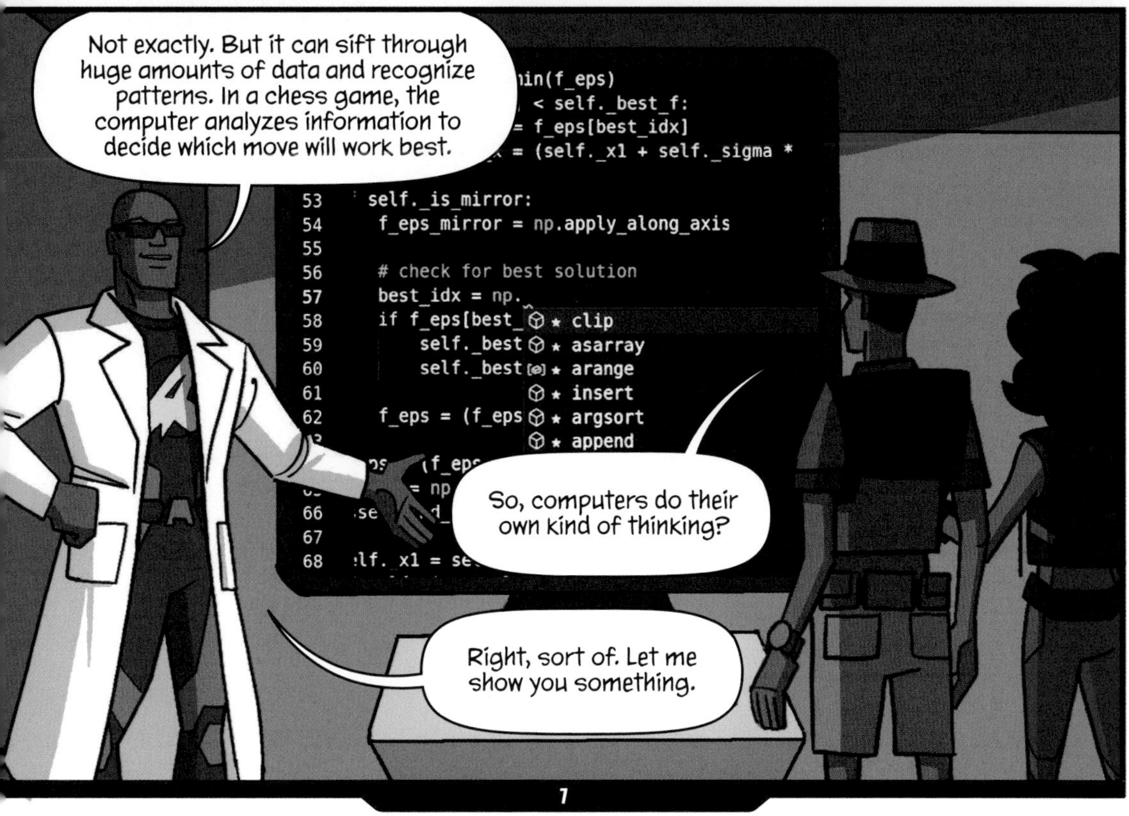
Not exactly. But it can sift through huge amounts of data and recognize patterns. In a chess game, the computer analyzes information to decide which move will work best.
min(f_eps)
< self._best_f:
= f_eps[best_idx]
= (self._x1 + self._sigma *
self._is_mirror:
f_eps_mirror = np.apply_along_axis
# check for best solution
best_idx = np.
if f_eps[best_
self._best
self._best
f_eps = (f_eps
clip
asarray
arange
insert
argsort
append
So, computers do their own kind of thinking?
Right, sort of. Let me show you something.

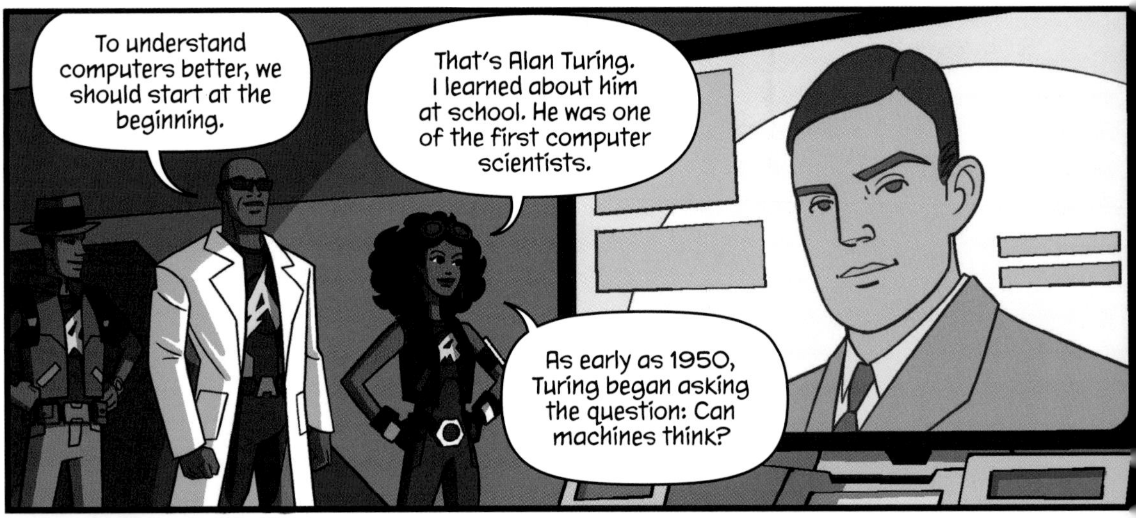
To understand computers better, we should start at the beginning.
That's Alan Turing. I learned about him at school. He was one of the first computer scientists.
As early as 1950, Turing began asking the question: Can machines think?

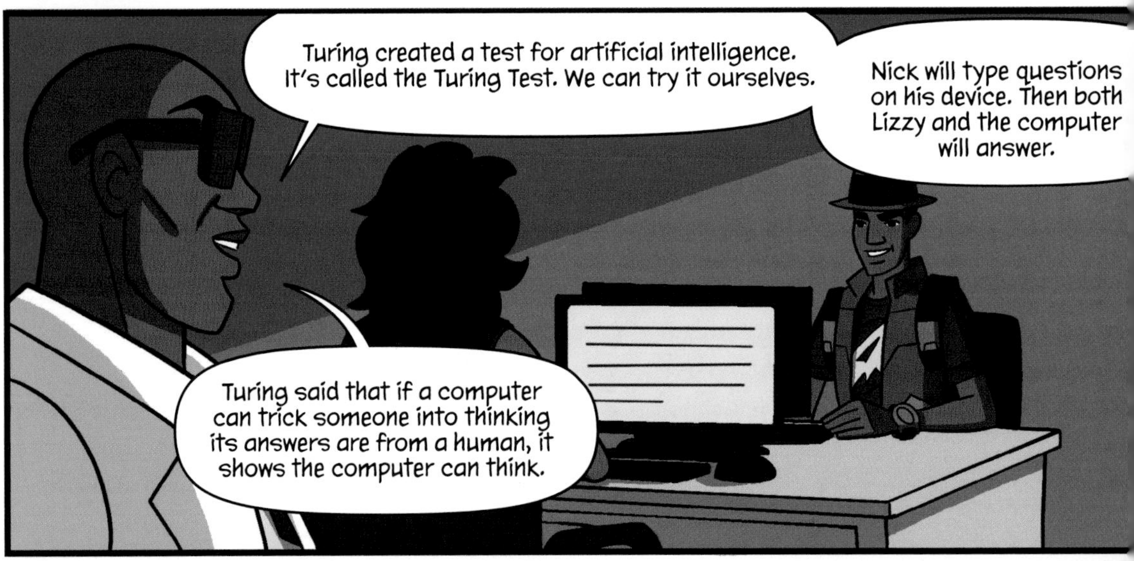
Turing created a test for artificial intelligence. It's called the Turing Test. We can try it ourselves.
Nick will type questions on his device. Then both Lizzy and the computer will answer.
Turing said that if a computer can trick someone into thinking its answers are from a human, it shows the computer can think.

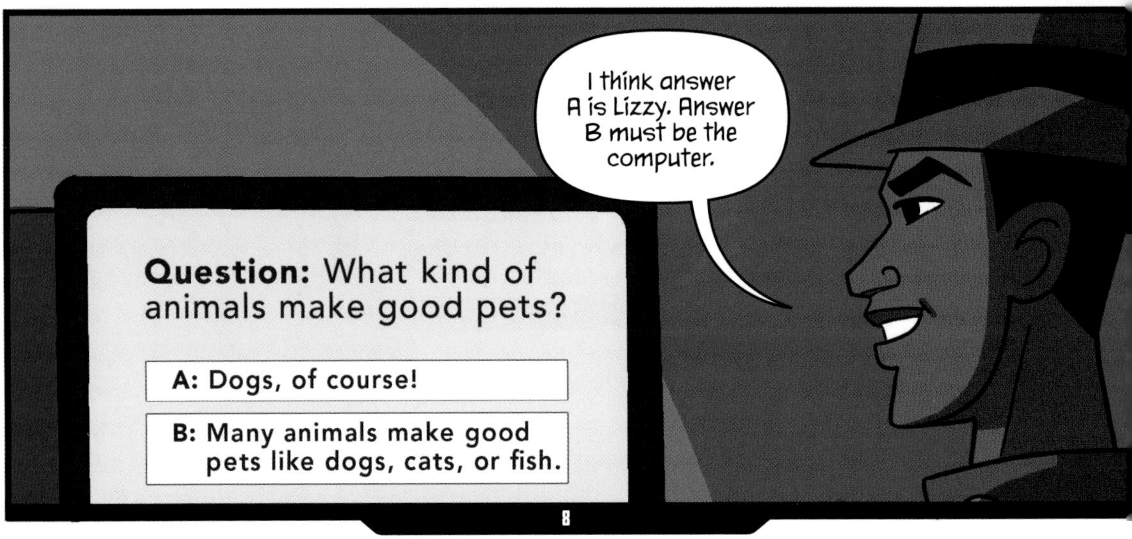
I think answer A is Lizzy. Answer B must be the computer.
Question: What kind of animals make good pets?
A: Dogs, of course!
B: Many animals make good pets like dogs, cats, or fish.

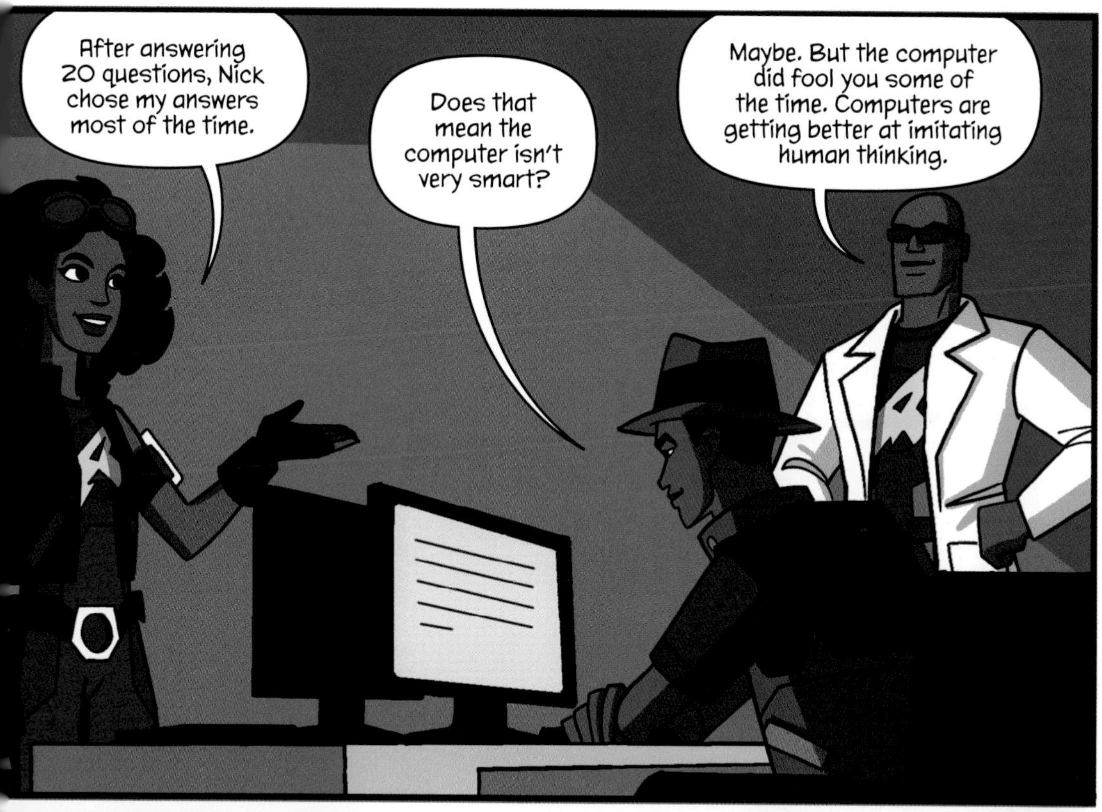
After answering 20 questions, Nick chose my answers most of the time.
Does that mean the computer isn't very smart?
Maybe. But the computer did fool you some of the time. Computers are getting better at imitating human thinking.

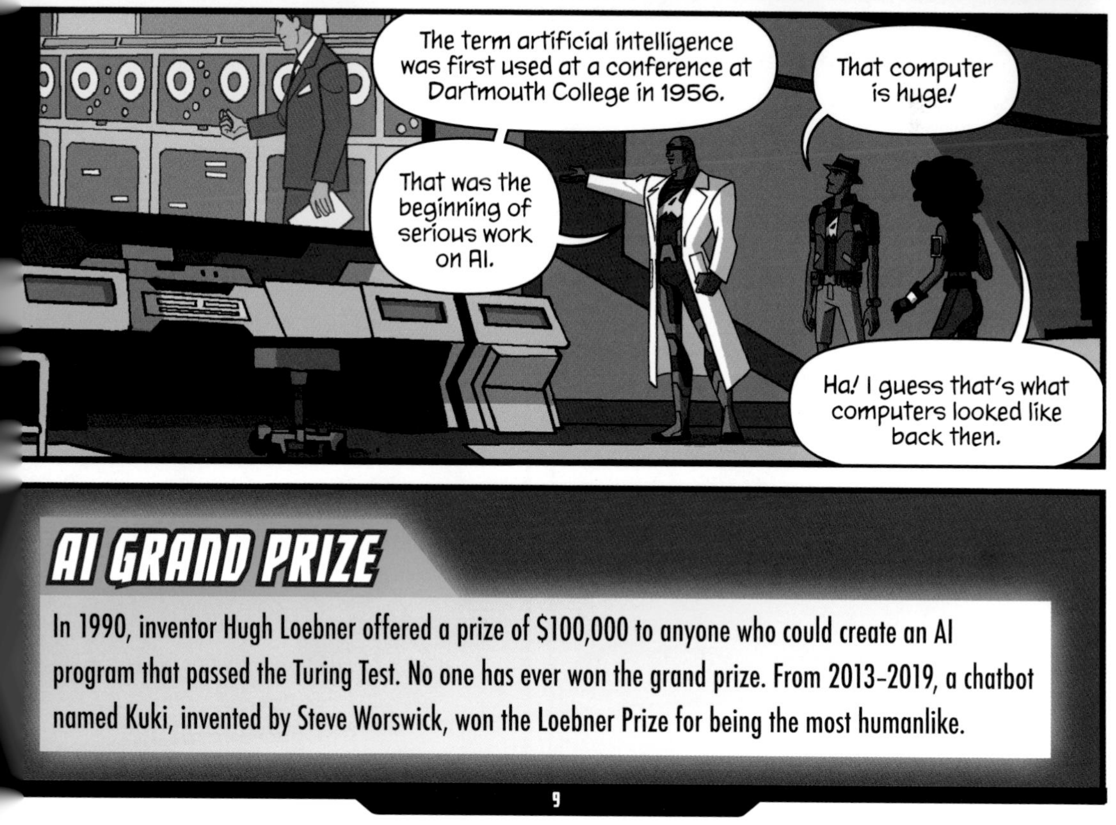
The term artificial intelligence was first used at a conference at Dartmouth College in 1956.
That was the beginning of serious work on AI.
That computer is huge!
Ha! I guess that's what computers looked like back then.

AI GRAND PRIZE

In 1990, inventor Hugh Loebner offered a prize of $100,000 to anyone who could create an AI program that passed the Turing Test. No one has ever won the grand prize. From 2013–2019, a chatbot named Kuki, invented by Steve Worswick, won the Loebner Prize for being the most humanlike.

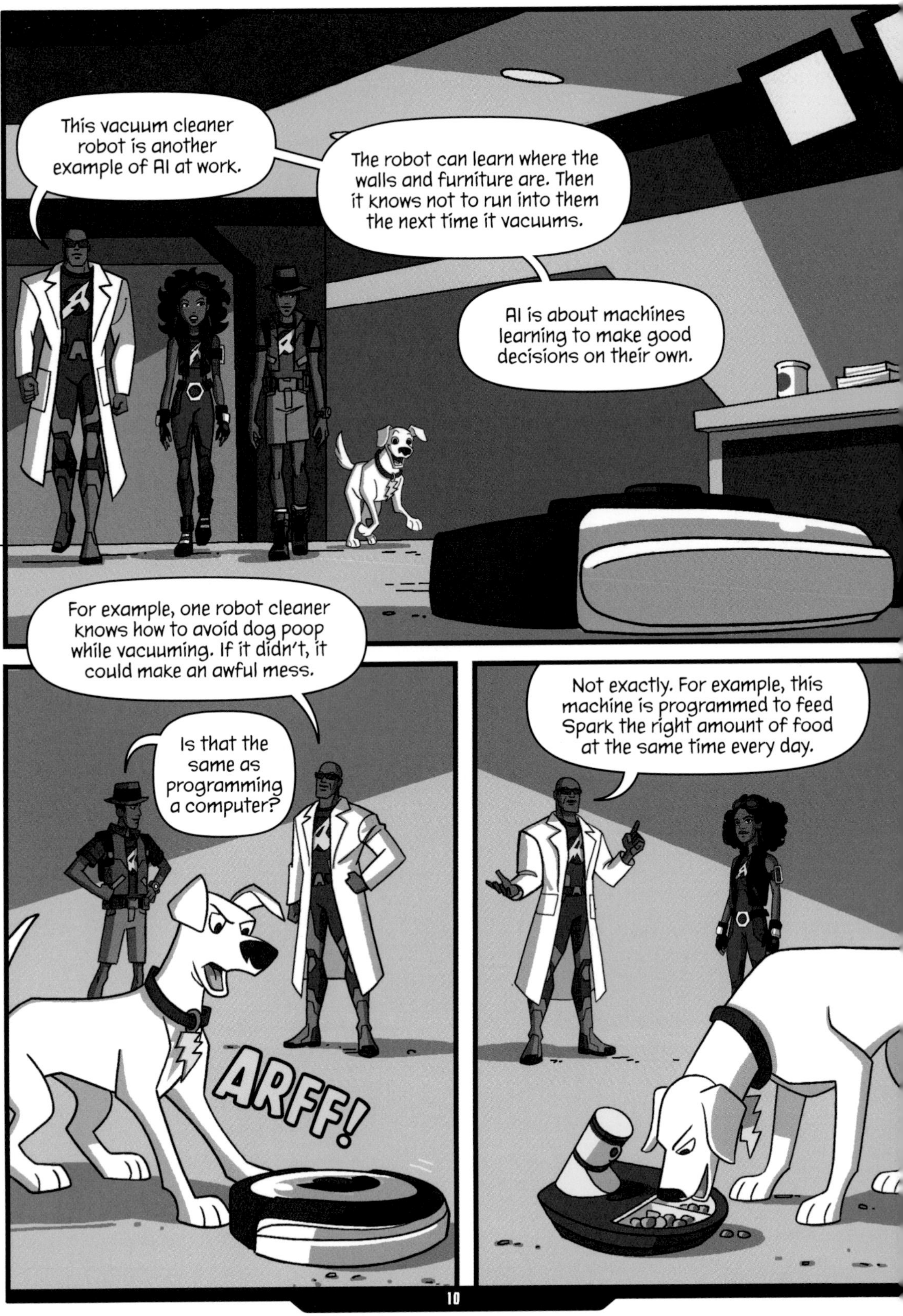

This vacuum cleaner robot is another example of AI at work.
The robot can learn where the walls and furniture are. Then it knows not to run into them the next time it vacuums.
AI is about machines learning to make good decisions on their own.
For example, one robot cleaner knows how to avoid dog poop while vacuuming. If it didn't, it could make an awful mess.
Is that the same as programming a computer?
ARFF!
Not exactly. For example, this machine is programmed to feed Spark the right amount of food at the same time every day.

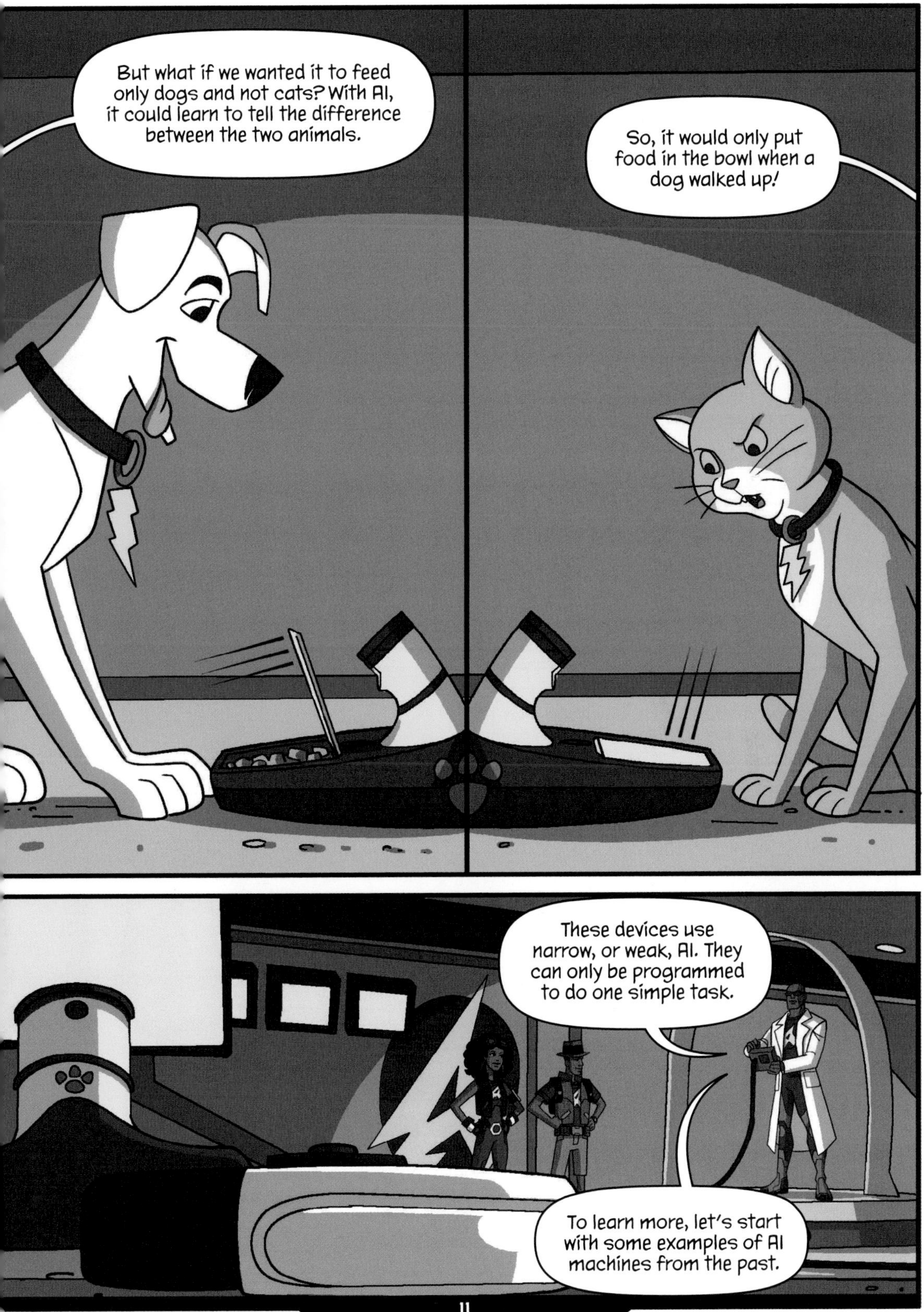
But what if we wanted it to feed only dogs and not cats? With AI, it could learn to tell the difference between the two animals.
So, it would only put food in the bowl when a dog walked up!
These devices use narrow, or weak, AI. They can only be programmed to do one simple task.
To learn more, let's start with some examples of AI machines from the past.

The first big breakthrough in AI came in 1997. The supercomputer Deep Blue beat chess master Gary Kasparov.

Another big step happened in 2011. A supercomputer named Watson beat the two biggest champions from the game show *Jeopardy!* after three matches.

$24,000

Who is Stoker?
(PER OW WELCOME OUR
MEW CHANTER OVERCRMS)
$1,000

$77,147

Who is Bram
Stoker?
$17,973

$21,600

WHO IS
BRAM STOKER?
$5600

It looks like the *Jeopardy!* champs were no contest for the computer.

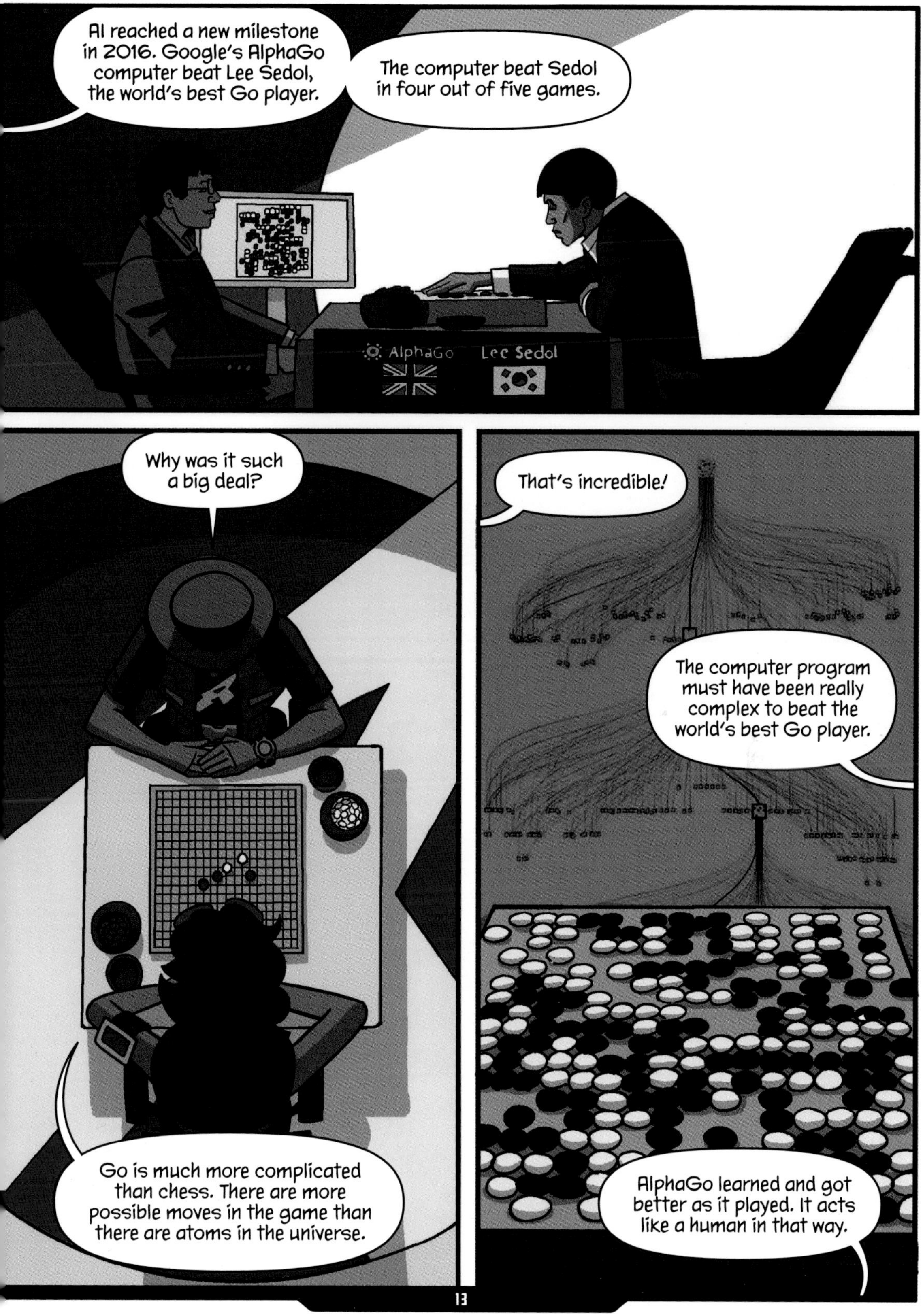
AI reached a new milestone in 2016. Google's AlphaGo computer beat Lee Sedol, the world's best Go player.
The computer beat Sedol in four out of five games.
AlphaGo
Lee Sedol
Why was it such a big deal?
Go is much more complicated than chess. There are more possible moves in the game than there are atoms in the universe.
That's incredible!
The computer program must have been really complex to beat the world's best Go player.
AlphaGo learned and got better as it played. It acts like a human in that way.

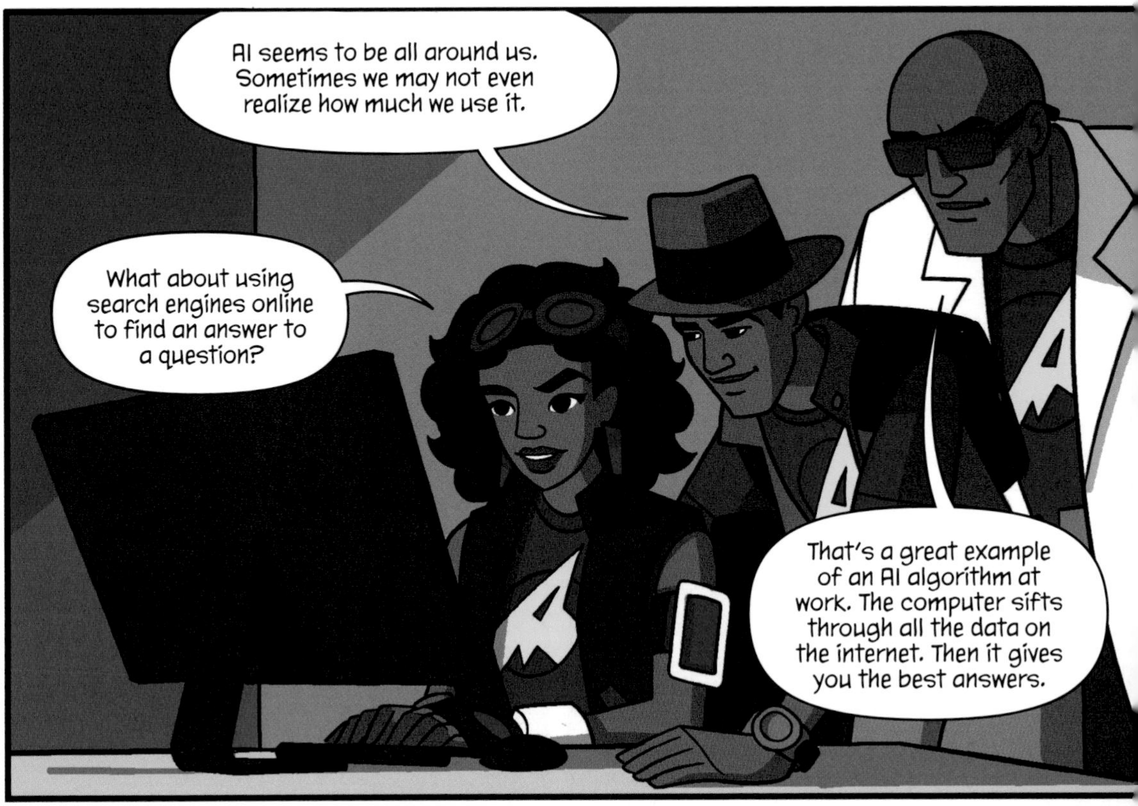
AI seems to be all around us. Sometimes we may not even realize how much we use it.
What about using search engines online to find an answer to a question?
That's a great example of an AI algorithm at work. The computer sifts through all the data on the internet. Then it gives you the best answers.

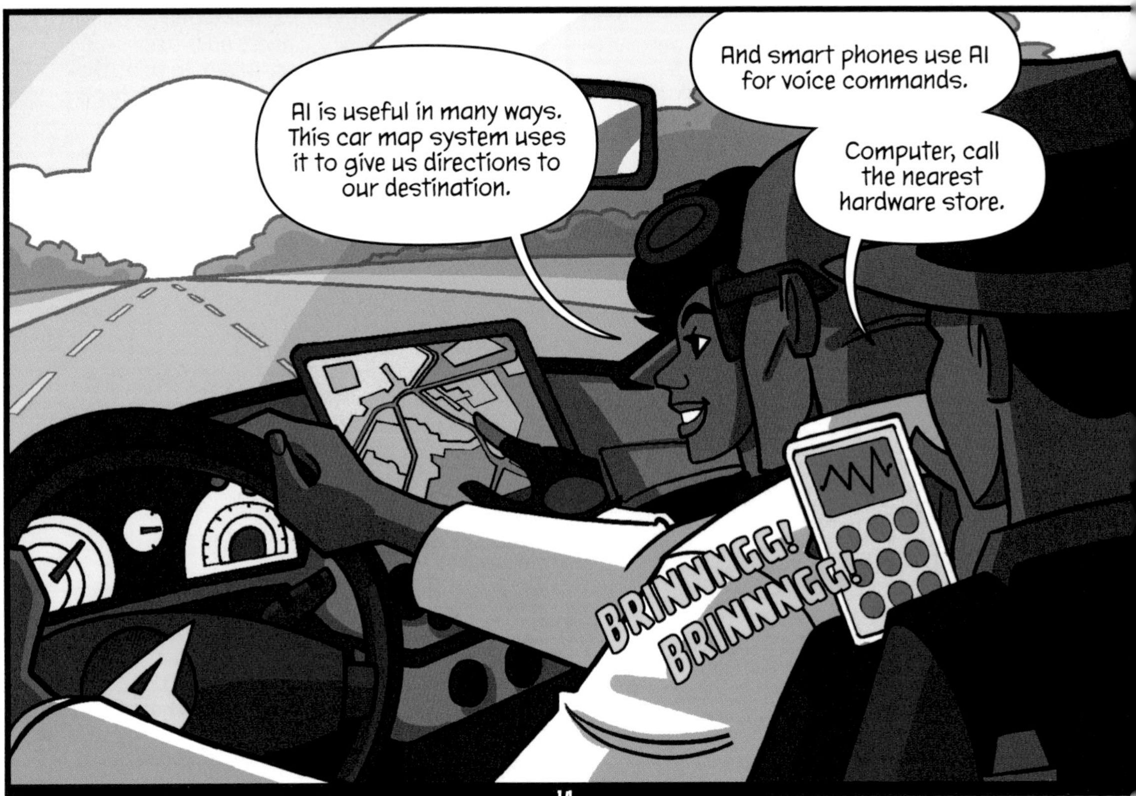
AI is useful in many ways. This car map system uses it to give us directions to our destination.
And smart phones use AI for voice commands.
Computer, call the nearest hardware store.
BRINNNGG! BRINNNGG!

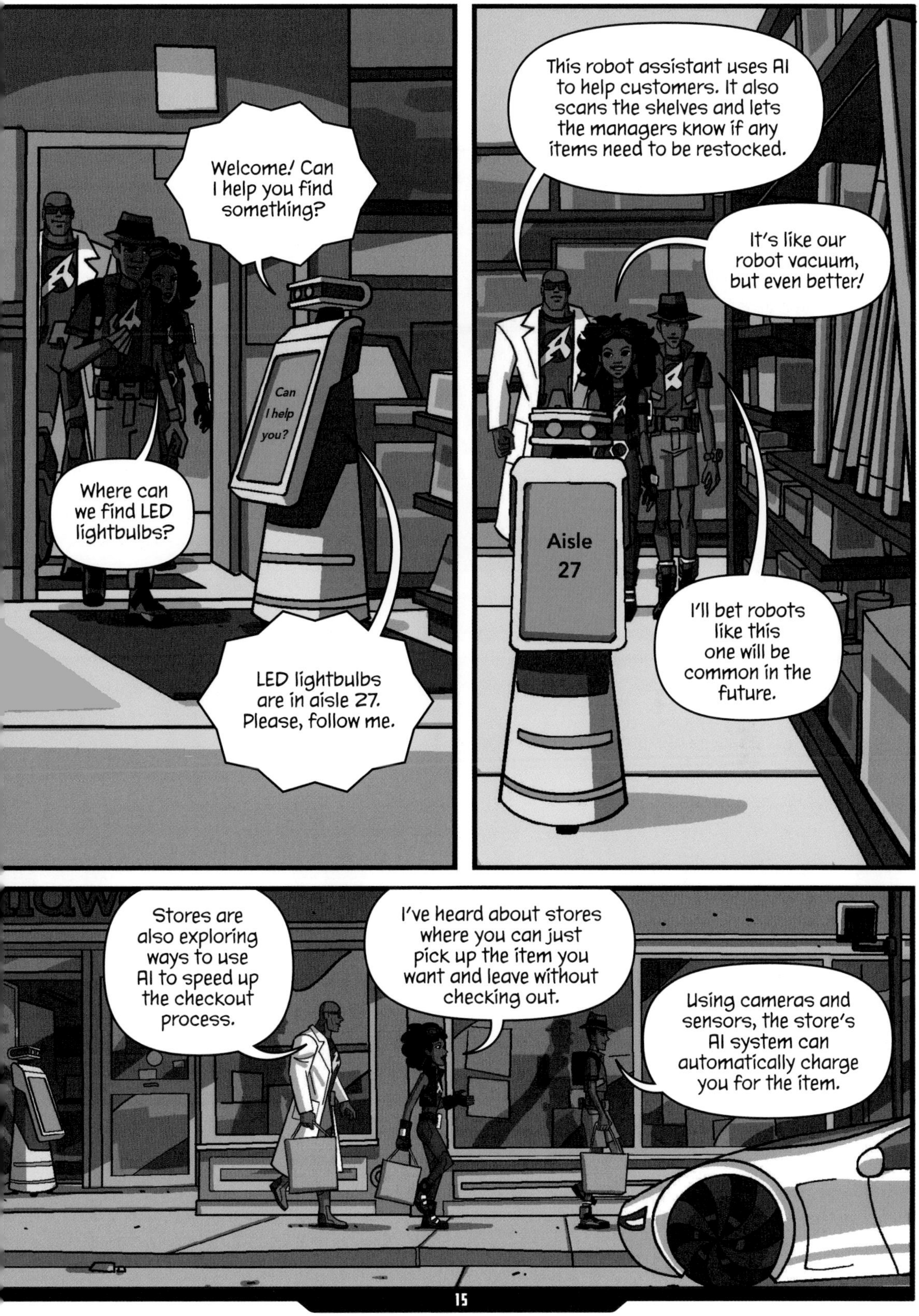
Welcome! Can I help you find something?
Can I help you?
Where can we find LED lightbulbs?
LED lightbulbs are in aisle 27. Please, follow me.
This robot assistant uses AI to help customers. It also scans the shelves and lets the managers know if any items need to be restocked.
It's like our robot vacuum, but even better!
Aisle 27
I'll bet robots like this one will be common in the future.
Stores are also exploring ways to use AI to speed up the checkout process.
I've heard about stores where you can just pick up the item you want and leave without checking out.
Using cameras and sensors, the store's AI system can automatically charge you for the item.

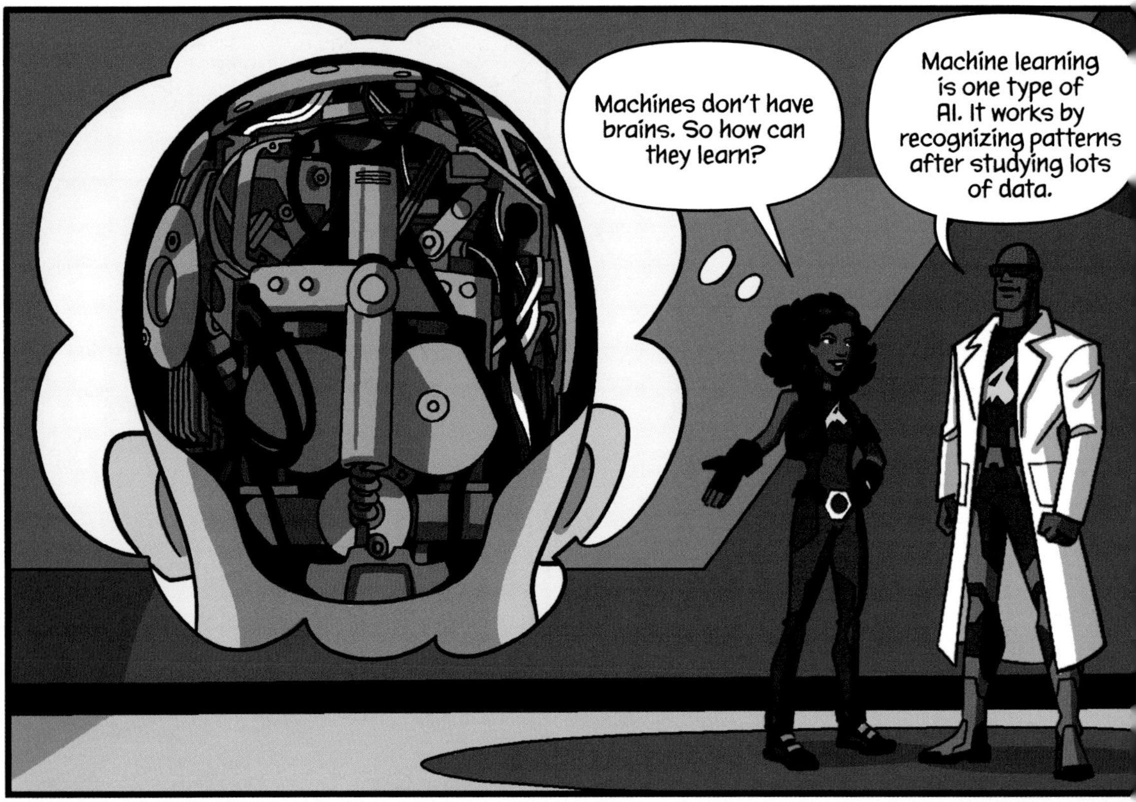
Machines don't have brains. So how can they learn?
Machine learning is one type of AI. It works by recognizing patterns after studying lots of data.

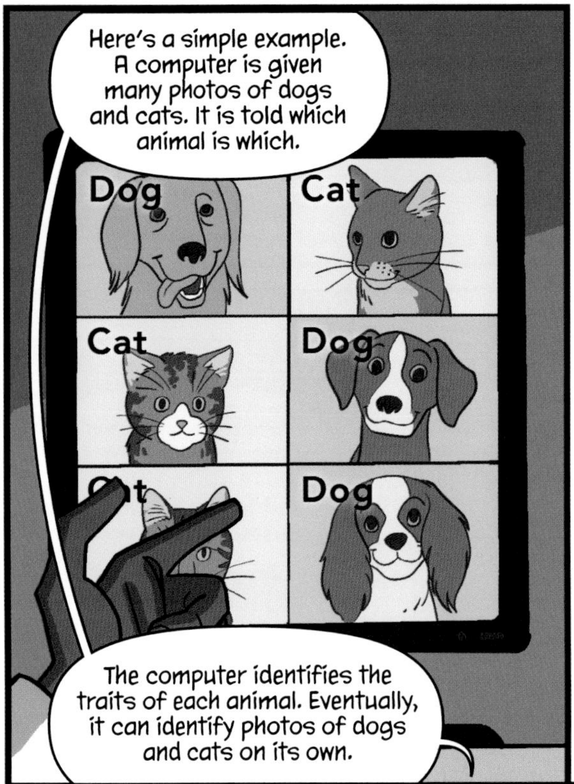
Here's a simple example. A computer is given many photos of dogs and cats. It is told which animal is which.
Dog
Cat
Cat
Dog
Dog
The computer identifies the traits of each animal. Eventually, it can identify photos of dogs and cats on its own.

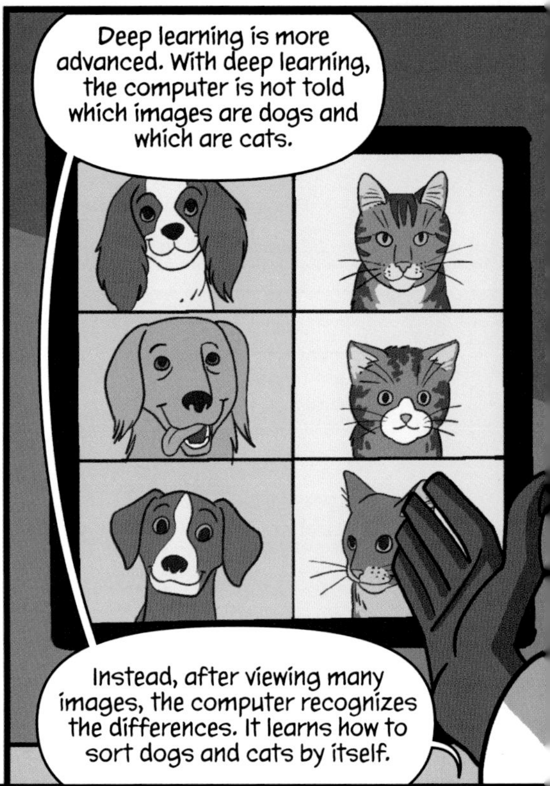
Deep learning is more advanced. With deep learning, the computer is not told which images are dogs and which are cats.
Instead, after viewing many images, the computer recognizes the differences. It learns how to sort dogs and cats by itself.

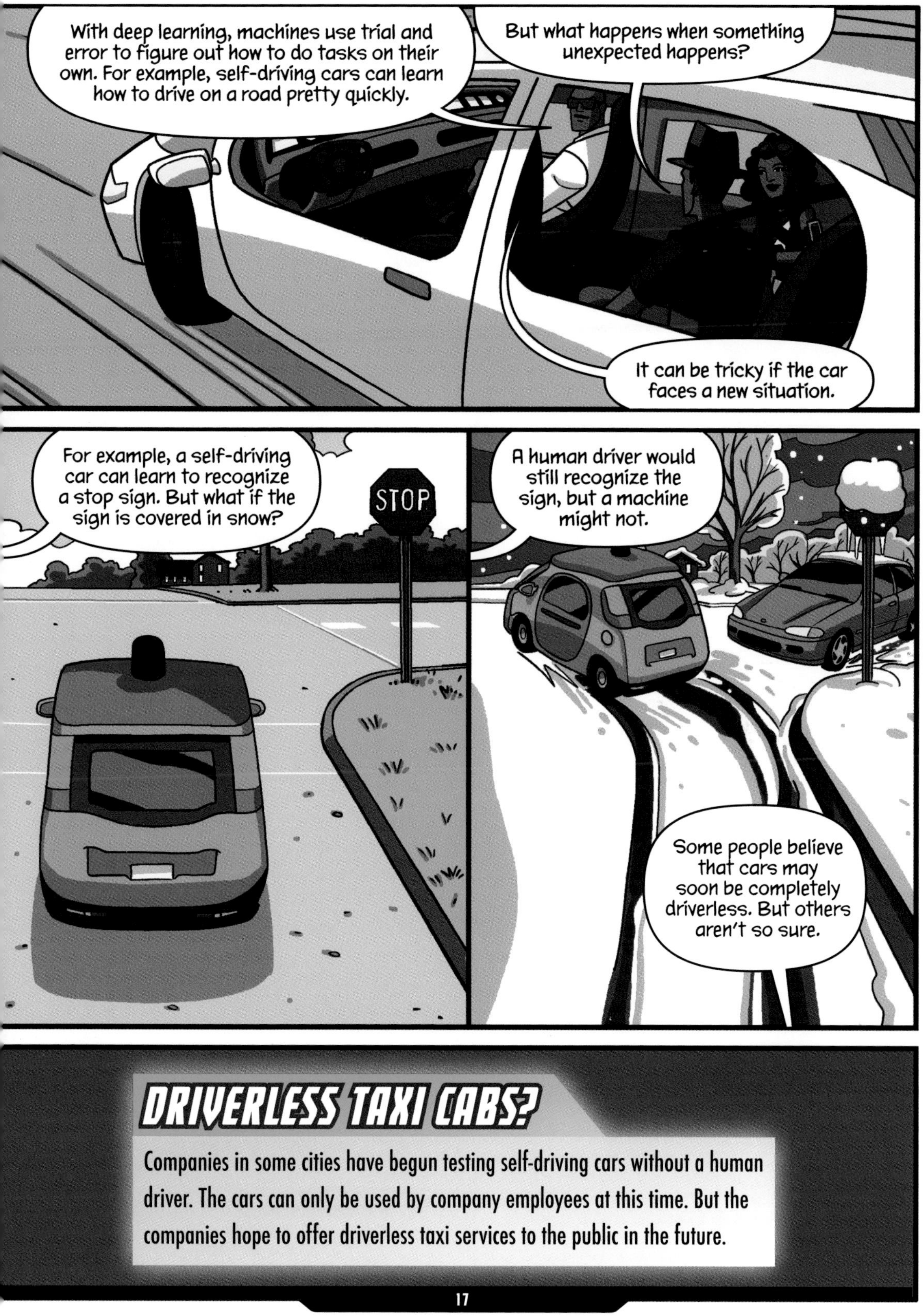

With deep learning, machines use trial and error to figure out how to do tasks on their own. For example, self-driving cars can learn how to drive on a road pretty quickly.
But what happens when something unexpected happens?
It can be tricky if the car faces a new situation.
For example, a self-driving car can learn to recognize a stop sign. But what if the sign is covered in snow?
STOP
A human driver would still recognize the sign, but a machine might not.
Some people believe that cars may soon be completely driverless. But others aren't so sure.

DRIVERLESS TAXI CABS?

Companies in some cities have begun testing self-driving cars without a human driver. The cars can only be used by company employees at this time. But the companies hope to offer driverless taxi services to the public in the future.

SECTION 3: *PROS AND CONS OF AI*

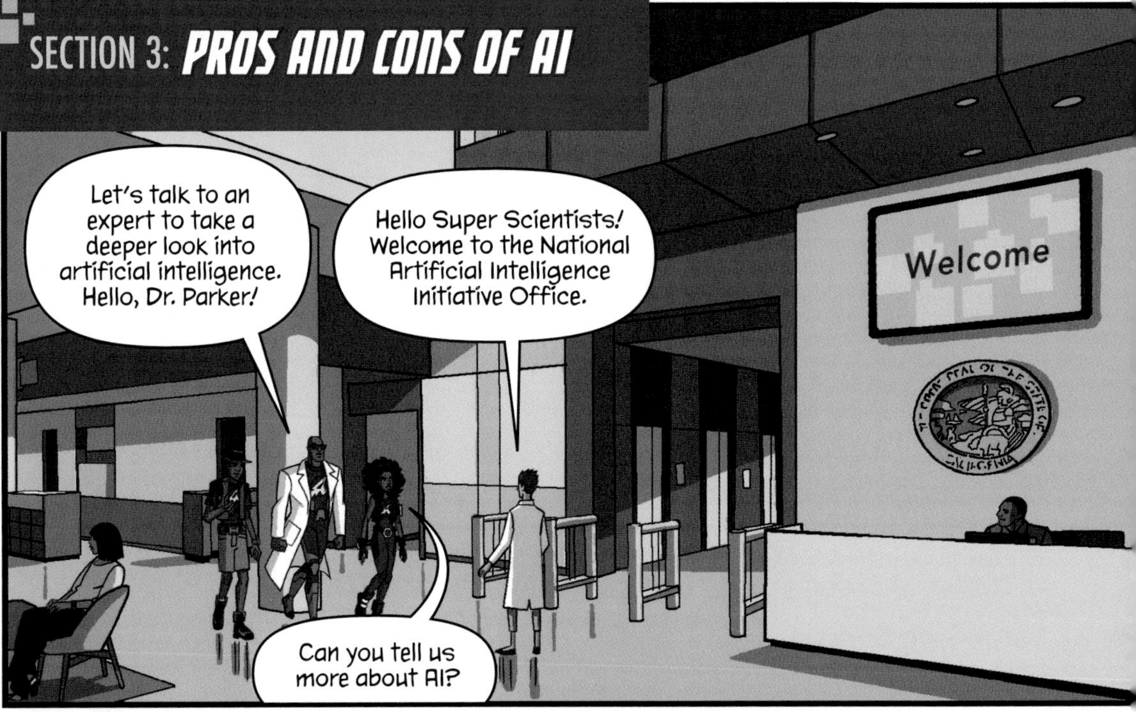
Let's talk to an expert to take a deeper look into artificial intelligence. Hello, Dr. Parker!
Hello Super Scientists! Welcome to the National Artificial Intelligence Initiative Office.
Welcome
Can you tell us more about AI?

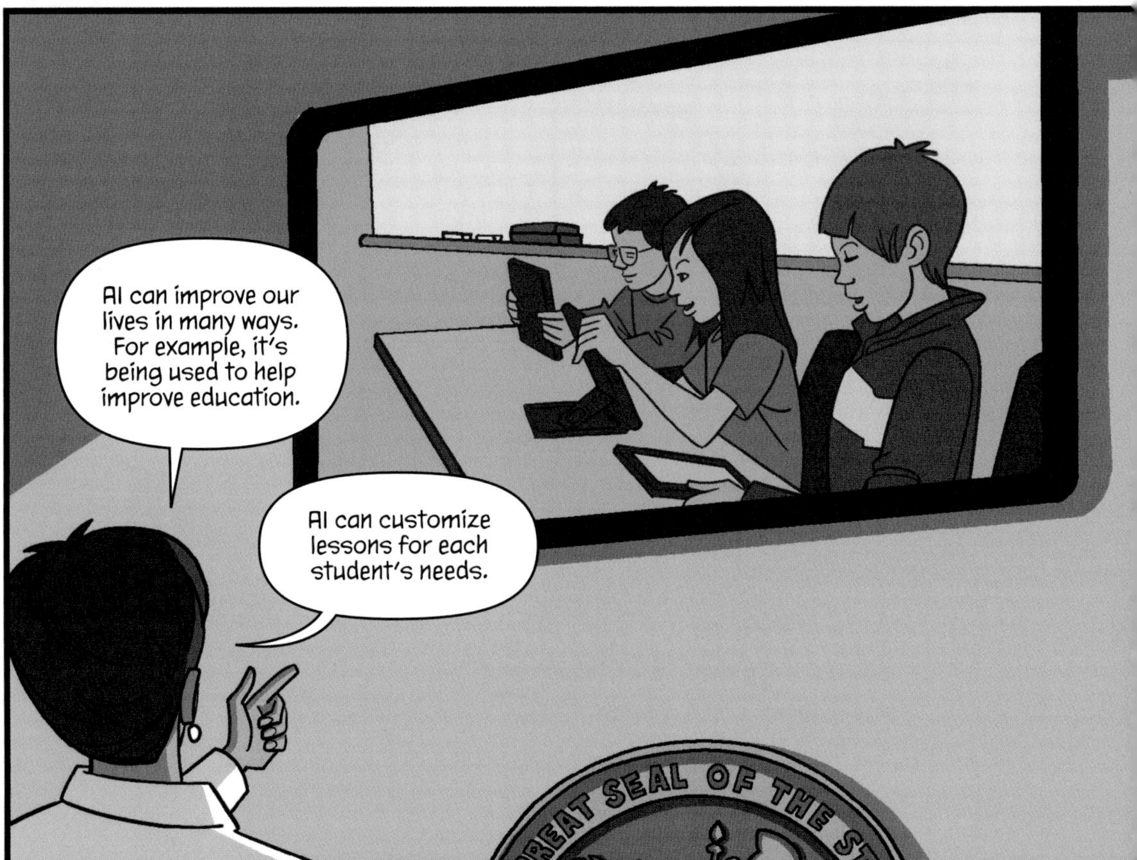
AI can improve our lives in many ways. For example, it's being used to help improve education.
AI can customize lessons for each student's needs.

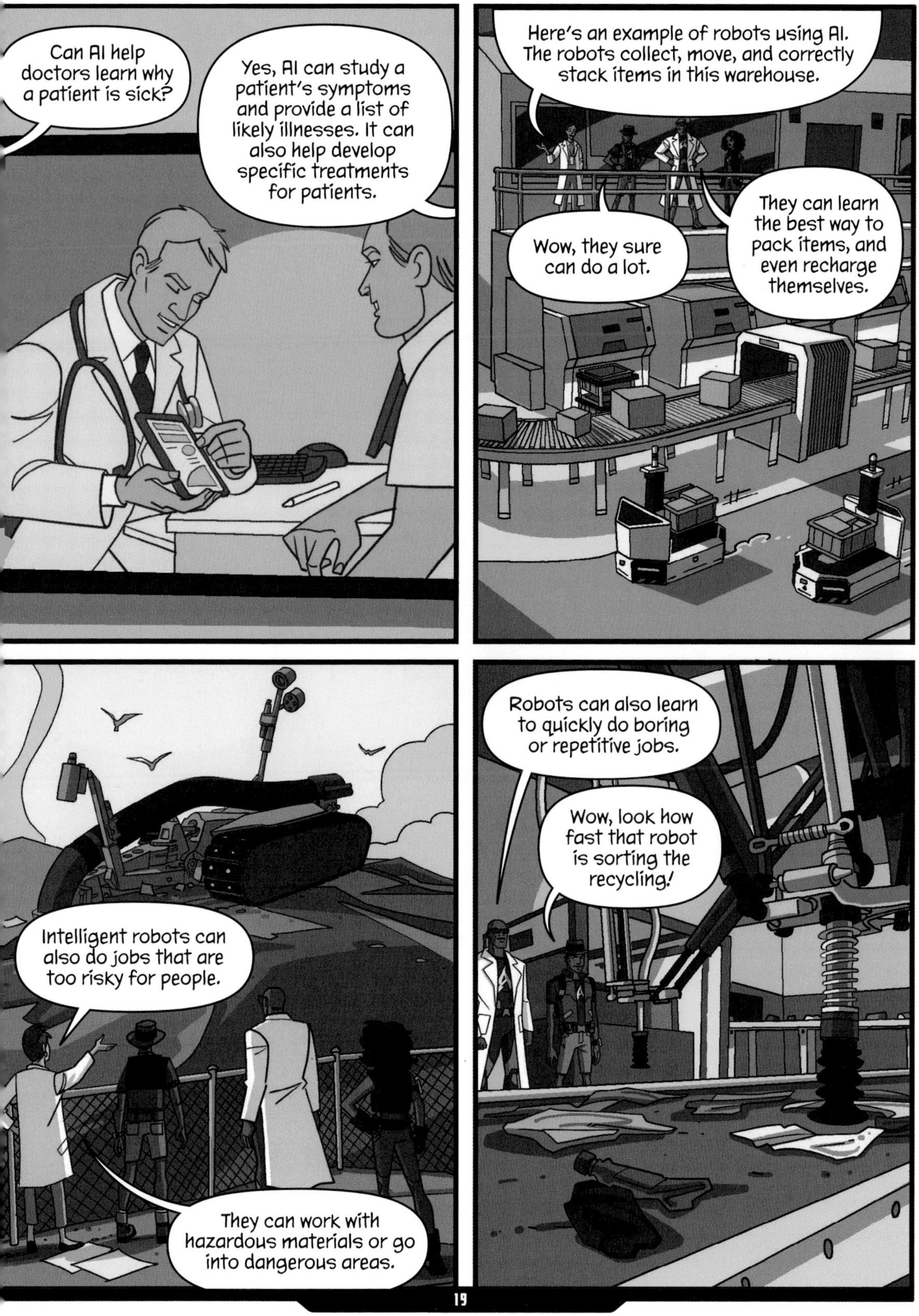
Can AI help doctors learn why a patient is sick?
Yes, AI can study a patient's symptoms and provide a list of likely illnesses. It can also help develop specific treatments for patients.
Here's an example of robots using AI. The robots collect, move, and correctly stack items in this warehouse.
Wow, they sure can do a lot.
They can learn the best way to pack items, and even recharge themselves.
Intelligent robots can also do jobs that are too risky for people.
They can work with hazardous materials or go into dangerous areas.
Robots can also learn to quickly do boring or repetitive jobs.
Wow, look how fast that robot is sorting the recycling!

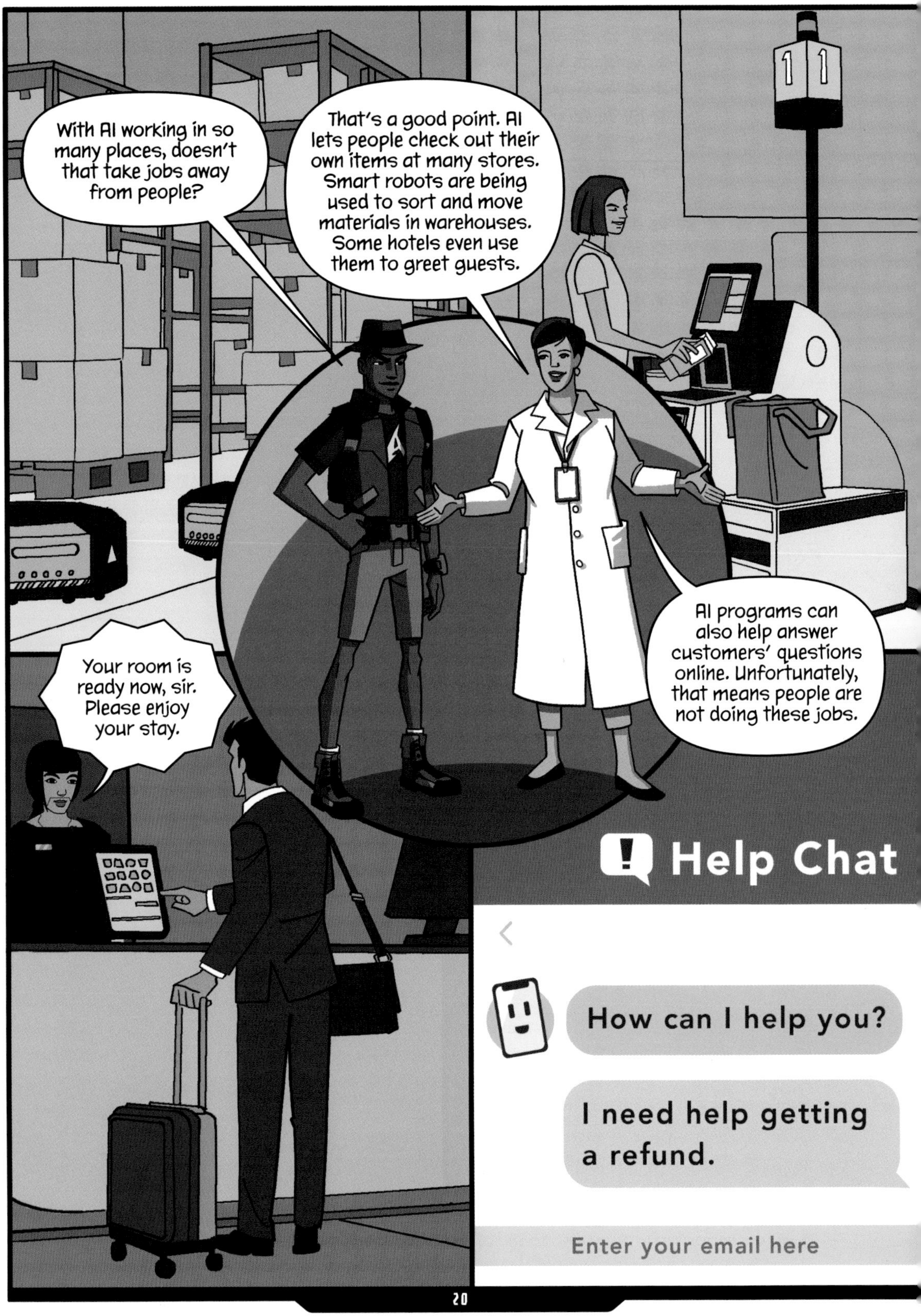
With AI working in so many places, doesn't that take jobs away from people?
That's a good point. AI lets people check out their own items at many stores. Smart robots are being used to sort and move materials in warehouses. Some hotels even use them to greet guests.
Your room is ready now, sir. Please enjoy your stay.
AI programs can also help answer customers' questions online. Unfortunately, that means people are not doing these jobs.
Help Chat
How can I help you?
I need help getting a refund.
Enter your email here

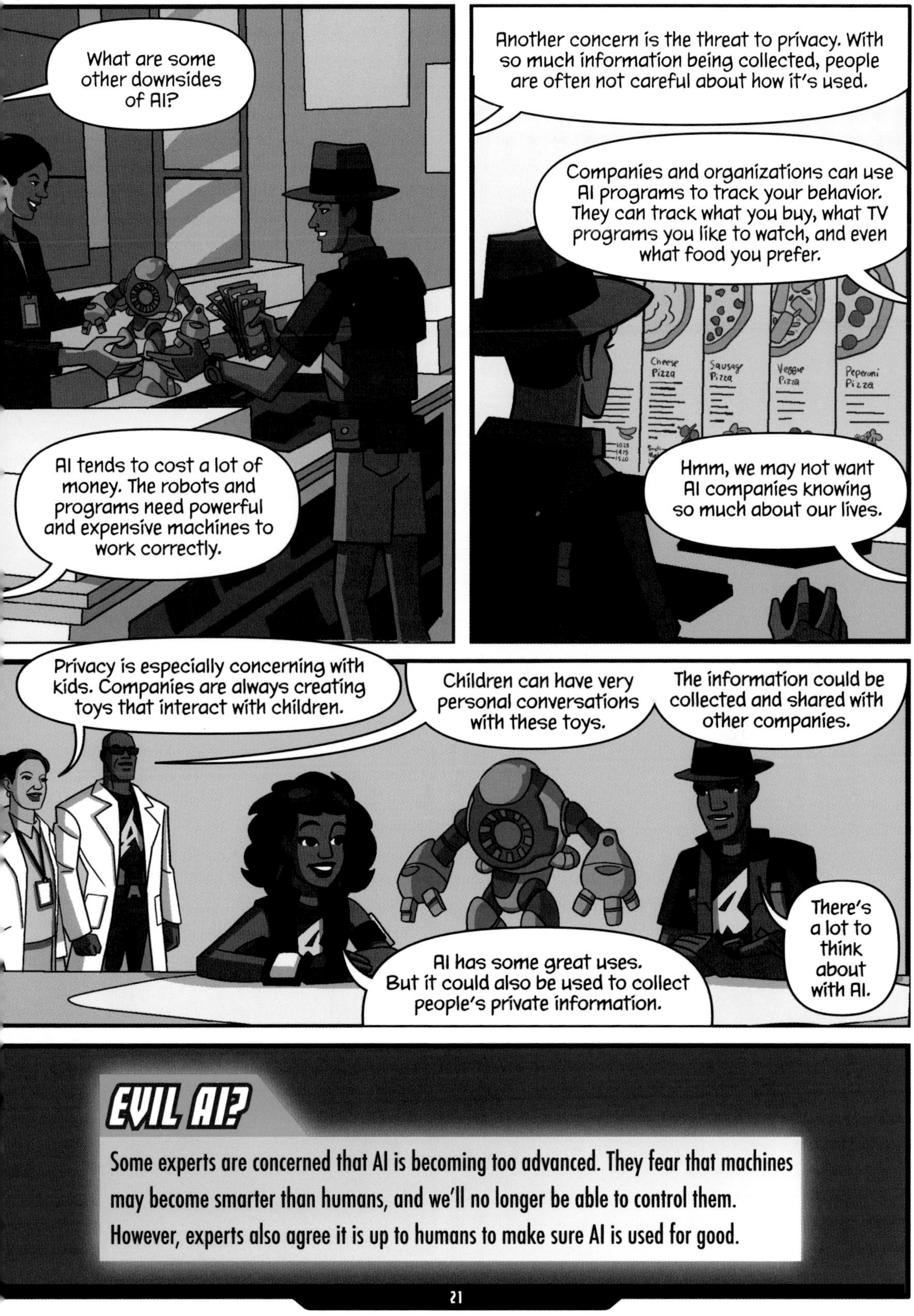
What are some other downsides of AI?
AI tends to cost a lot of money. The robots and programs need powerful and expensive machines to work correctly.
Another concern is the threat to privacy. With so much information being collected, people are often not careful about how it's used.
Companies and organizations can use AI programs to track your behavior. They can track what you buy, what TV programs you like to watch, and even what food you prefer.
Cheese Pizza
Sausage Pizza
Veggie Pizza
Peperoni Pizza
Hmm, we may not want AI companies knowing so much about our lives.
Privacy is especially concerning with kids. Companies are always creating toys that interact with children.
Children can have very personal conversations with these toys.
The information could be collected and shared with other companies.
AI has some great uses. But it could also be used to collect people's private information.
There's a lot to think about with AI.

EVIL AI?

Some experts are concerned that AI is becoming too advanced. They fear that machines may become smarter than humans, and we'll no longer be able to control them. However, experts also agree it is up to humans to make sure AI is used for good.

SECTION 4: *THE FUTURE OF AI*

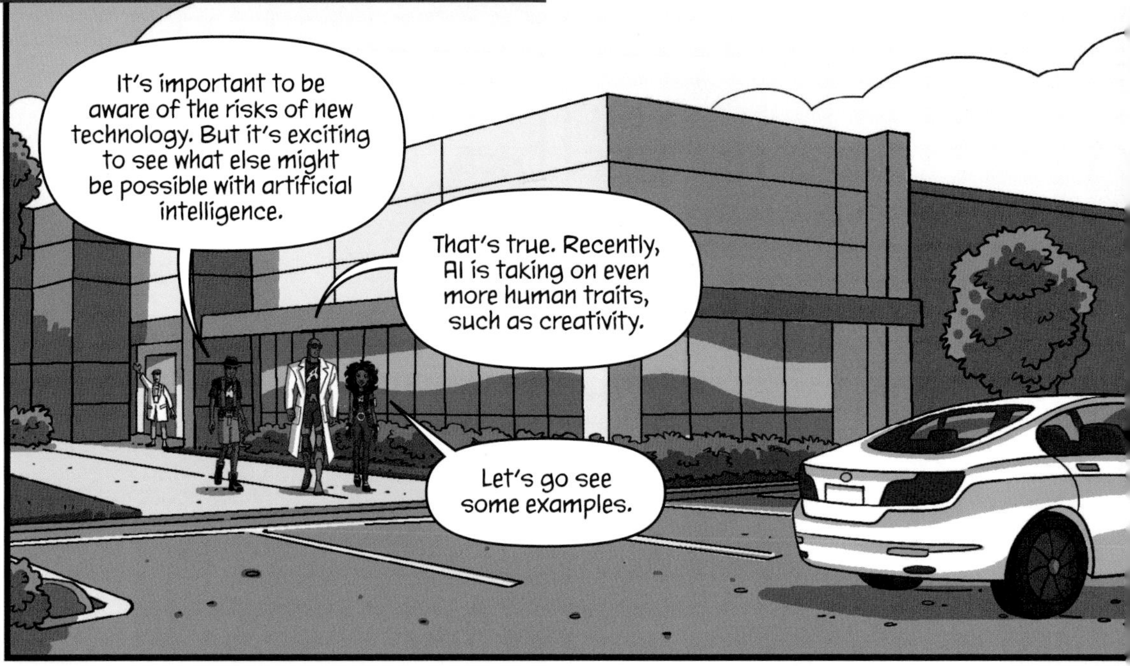
It's important to be aware of the risks of new technology. But it's exciting to see what else might be possible with artificial intelligence.
That's true. Recently, AI is taking on even more human traits, such as creativity.
Let's go see some examples.

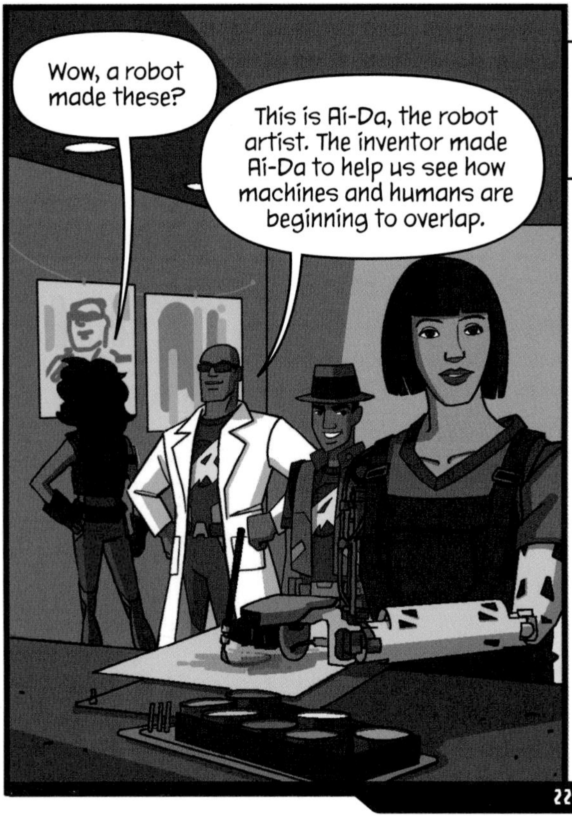
Wow, a robot made these?
This is Ai-Da, the robot artist. The inventor made Ai-Da to help us see how machines and humans are beginning to overlap.

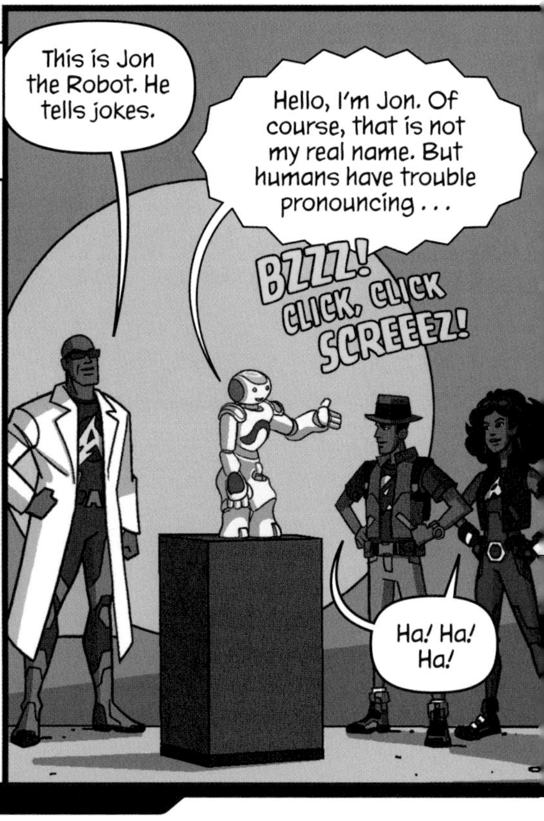
This is Jon the Robot. He tells jokes.
Hello, I'm Jon. Of course, that is not my real name. But humans have trouble pronouncing . . .
BZZZ! CLICK, CLICK SCREEEZ!
Ha! Ha! Ha!

I didn't know that robots can have a sense of humor.

Jon's inventor actually wrote the jokes.

However, the robot is learning to adjust the timing of the jokes based on the response from the audience.

That's so interesting. It uses AI to become a better comedian.

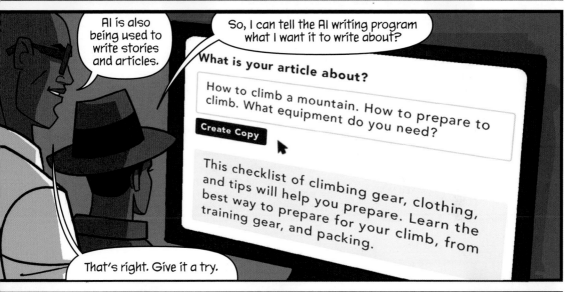

AI is also being used to write stories and articles.

So, I can tell the AI writing program what I want it to write about?

What is your article about?

How to climb a mountain. How to prepare to climb. What equipment do you need?

Create Copy

This checklist of climbing gear, clothing, and tips will help you prepare. Learn the best way to prepare for your climb, from training gear, and packing.

That's right. Give it a try.

The computer's writing was pretty good.

With AI, the output depends on what is put into it first.

But what if the information is put into the program the wrong way?

That could cause problems.

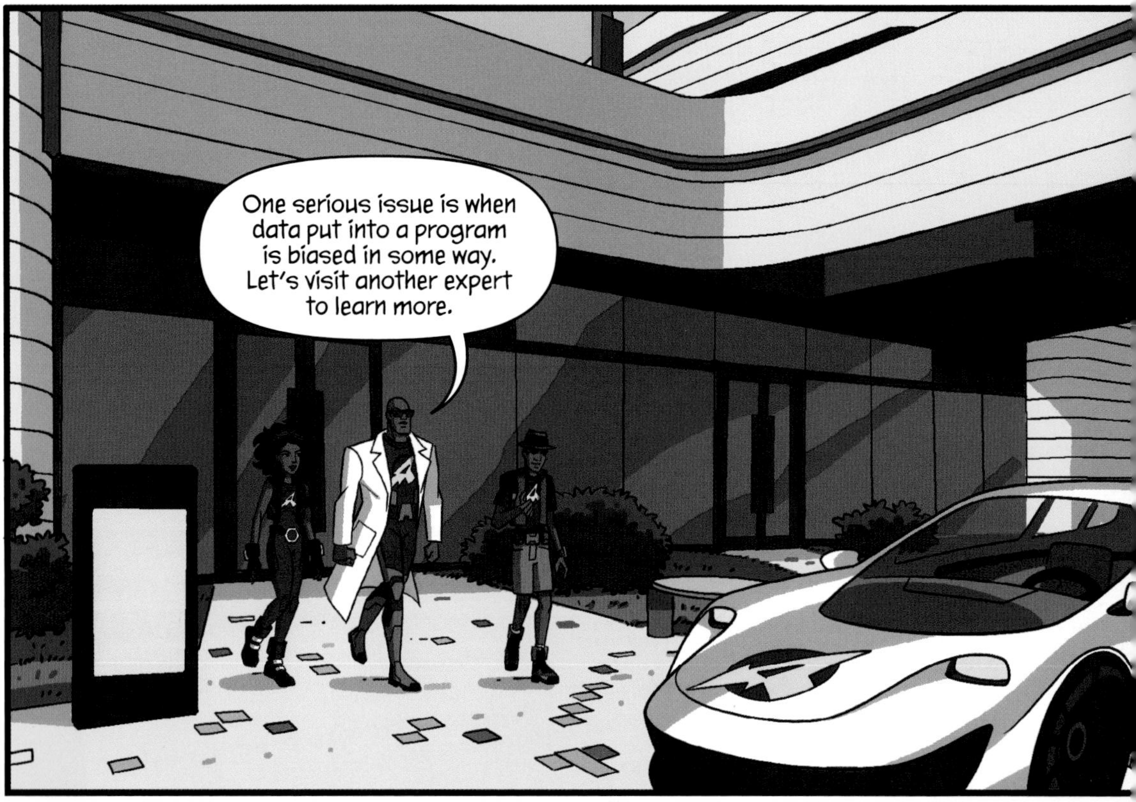
One serious issue is when data put into a program is biased in some way. Let's visit another expert to learn more.

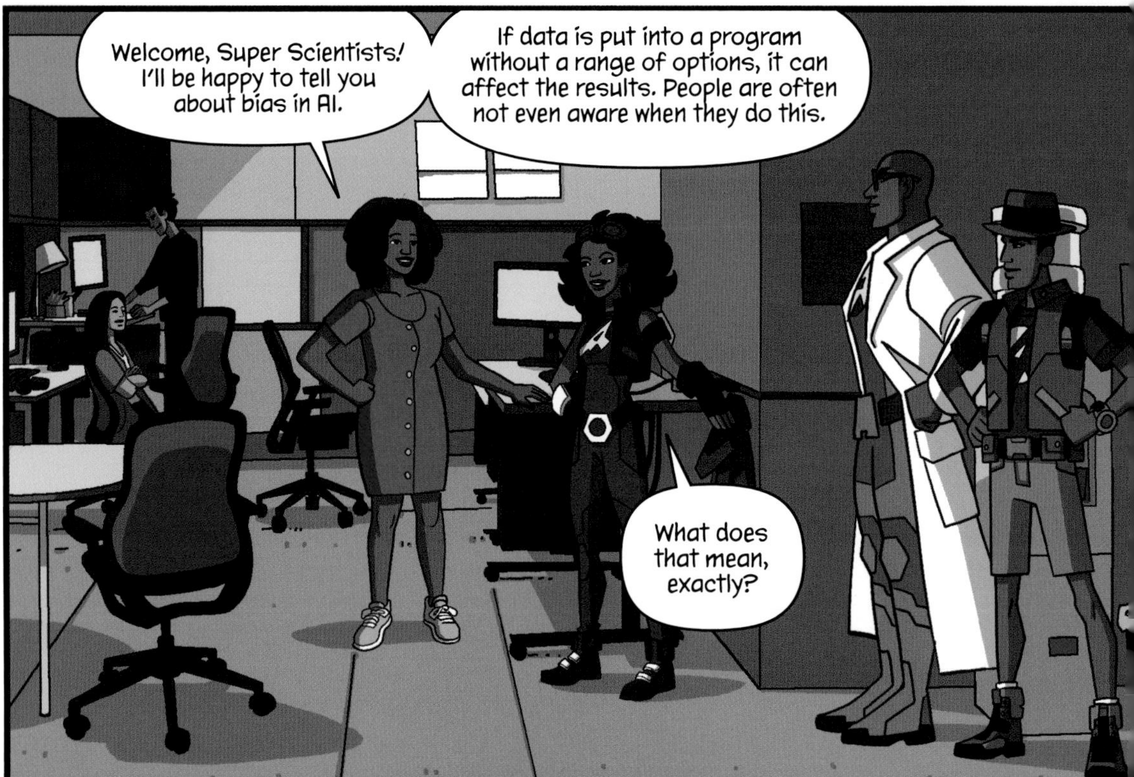
Welcome, Super Scientists! I'll be happy to tell you about bias in AI.
If data is put into a program without a range of options, it can affect the results. People are often not even aware when they do this.
What does that mean, exactly?

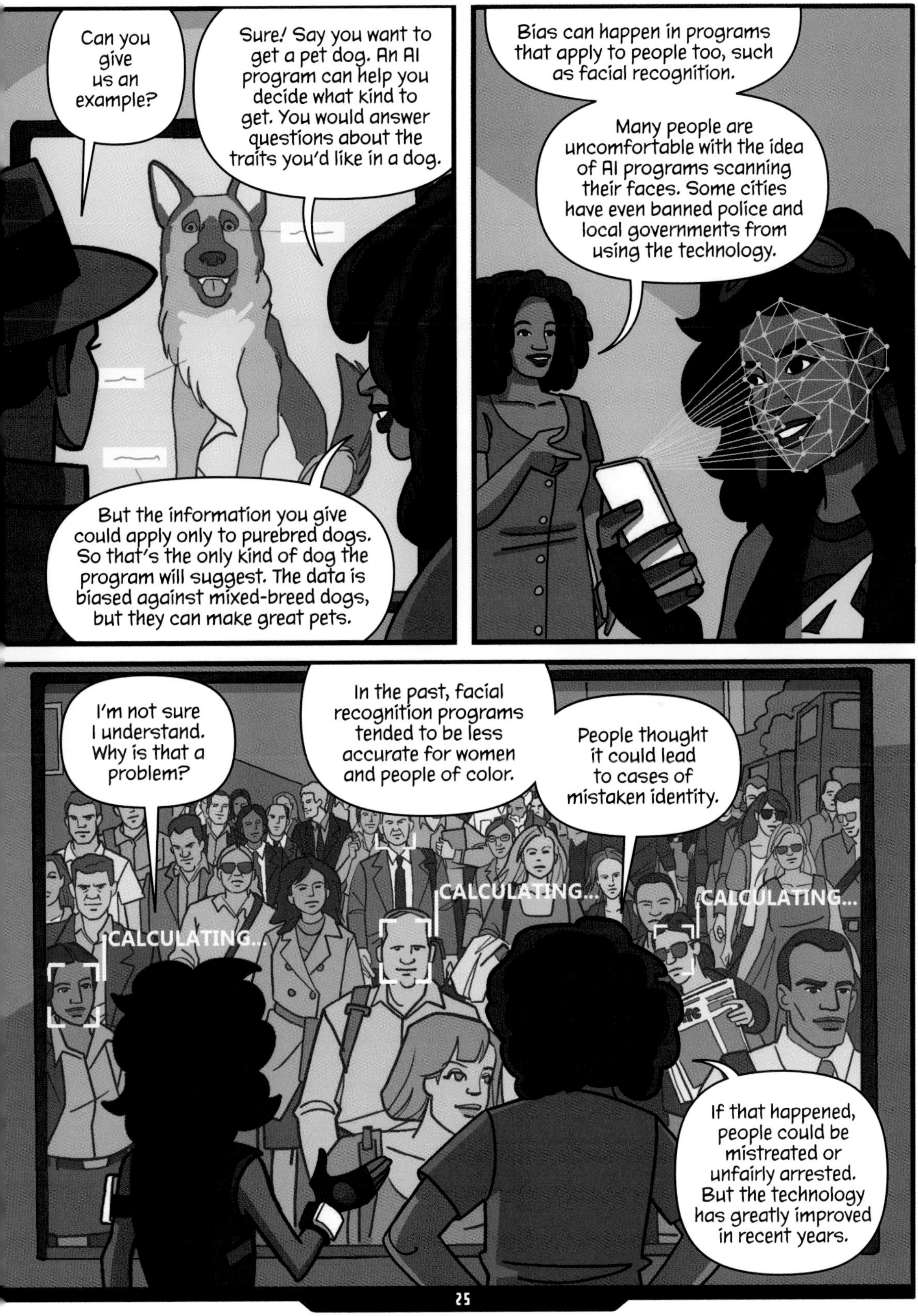

Can you give us an example?
Sure! Say you want to get a pet dog. An AI program can help you decide what kind to get. You would answer questions about the traits you'd like in a dog.
But the information you give could apply only to purebred dogs. So that's the only kind of dog the program will suggest. The data is biased against mixed-breed dogs, but they can make great pets.
Bias can happen in programs that apply to people too, such as facial recognition.
Many people are uncomfortable with the idea of AI programs scanning their faces. Some cities have even banned police and local governments from using the technology.
I'm not sure I understand. Why is that a problem?
In the past, facial recognition programs tended to be less accurate for women and people of color.
People thought it could lead to cases of mistaken identity.
CALCULATING...
CALCULATING...
CALCULATING...
If that happened, people could be mistreated or unfairly arrested. But the technology has greatly improved in recent years.

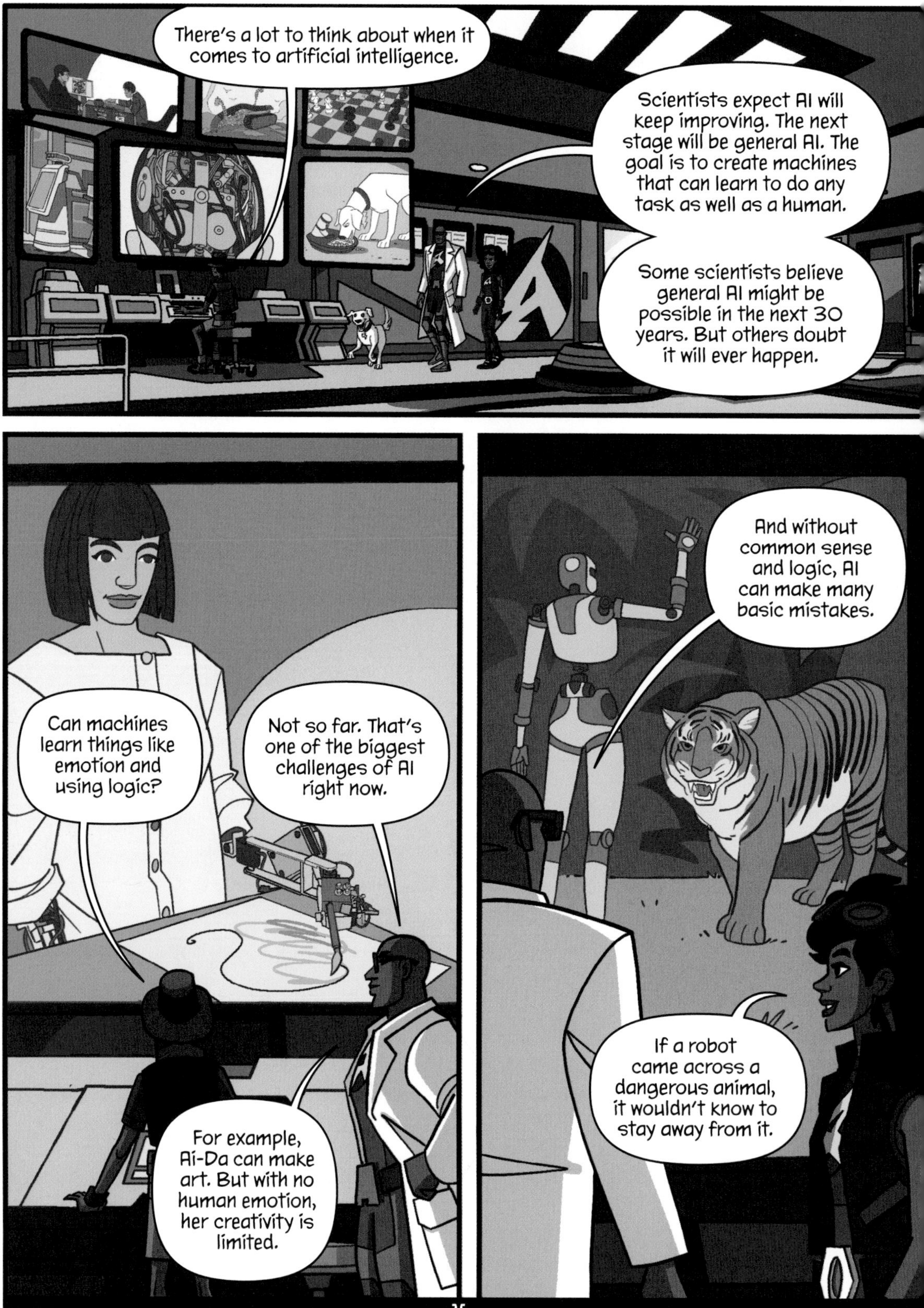
There's a lot to think about when it comes to artificial intelligence.
Scientists expect AI will keep improving. The next stage will be general AI. The goal is to create machines that can learn to do any task as well as a human.
Some scientists believe general AI might be possible in the next 30 years. But others doubt it will ever happen.
Can machines learn things like emotion and using logic?
Not so far. That's one of the biggest challenges of AI right now.
For example, Ai-Da can make art. But with no human emotion, her creativity is limited.
And without common sense and logic, AI can make many basic mistakes.
If a robot came across a dangerous animal, it wouldn't know to stay away from it.

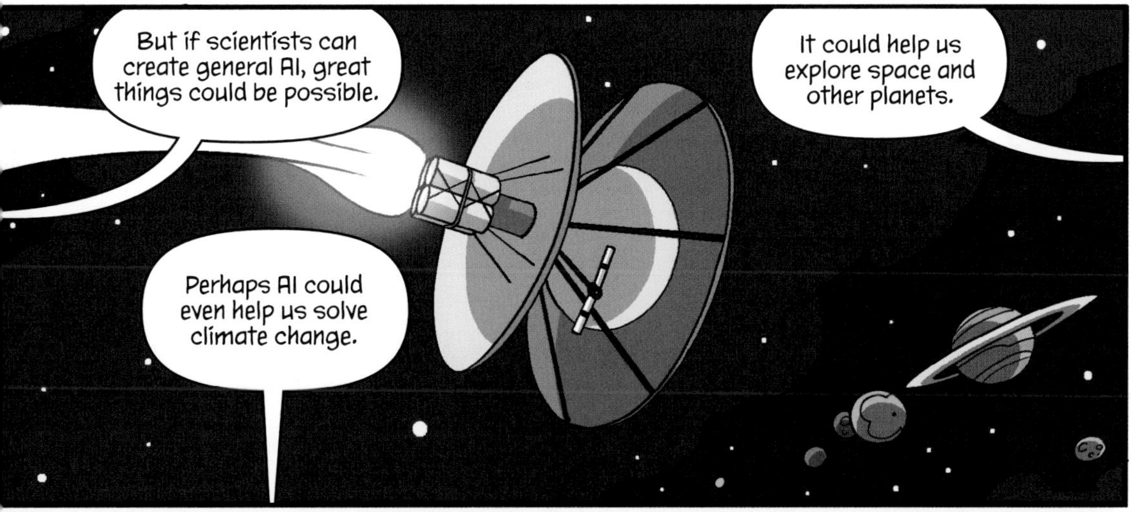

But if scientists can create general AI, great things could be possible.
It could help us explore space and other planets.
Perhaps AI could even help us solve climate change.

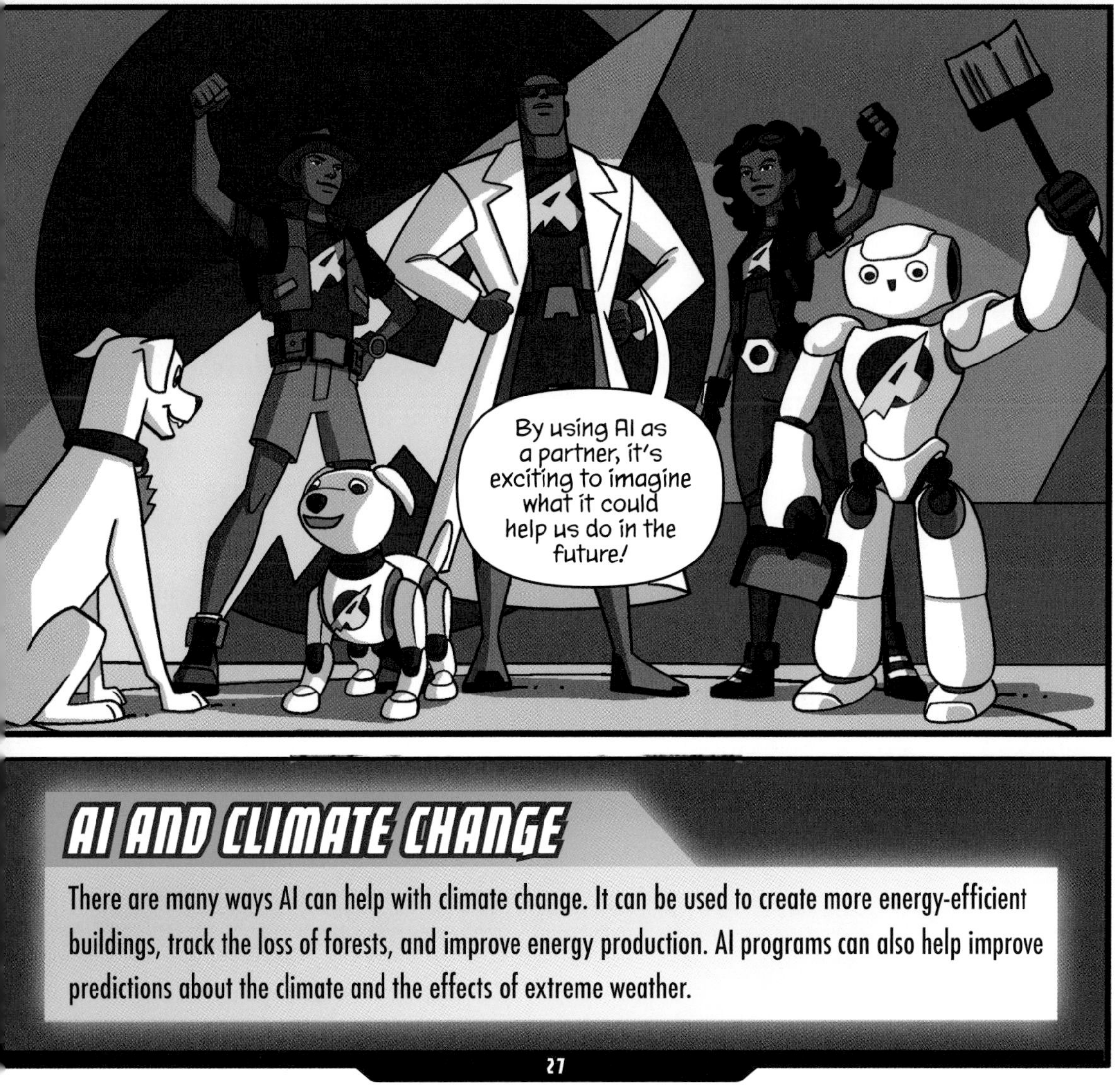

By using AI as a partner, it's exciting to imagine what it could help us do in the future!

AI AND CLIMATE CHANGE

There are many ways AI can help with climate change. It can be used to create more energy-efficient buildings, track the loss of forests, and improve energy production. AI programs can also help improve predictions about the climate and the effects of extreme weather.

MORE ABOUT ARTIFICIAL INTELLIGENCE

Scientists and engineers are working on creating robots that can help solve unique and challenging problems. Artificial intelligence has opened doors to some exciting possibilities.

Many people are concerned about keeping ocean animals captive in marine parks. One company has developed a solution. They created a robot dolphin that's so lifelike that it's hard to tell it apart from the real thing. These robot dolphins could one day replace real dolphins in marine parks.

A company in the Netherlands has created a robot bird that looks and flies like a Peregrine falcon. It was invented to help solve the problem of birds damaging large airplane engines. The robot falcon scares real birds away from aircraft that are getting ready to take off.

Rats are rarely seen as helpful, but a robot rat may one day save lives. This robot rodent can squeeze into narrow spaces, climb, get past obstacles, and walk on snow. The robot's creators hope it can be used after disasters, such as earthquakes. It could reach survivors and bring them supplies until they can be rescued.

Robots are being developed to be companions for older people. Some can do tasks such as cleaning, fetching items, and reminding people to take their medication. Others can have conversations or even play card games with people. With the help of robots, many older people could continue living independently in their homes.

Several companies are working on devices that can help the blind and visually impaired. The devices use cameras to view the user's surroundings. The devices then describe what they see in detail through an earpiece worn by the user. These smart devices can read text and signs, guide people to their destinations, and even recognize people.

GLOSSARY

algorithm (AL-guh-rith-uhm)—a set of step-by-step instructions used to process data and solve a problem or accomplish a goal

bias (BYE-uhs)—a tendency to favor one position or point of view over another

data (DAY-tuh)—information or facts that can be used to analyze or solve a problem

facial recognition (FAY-shul rek-uhg-NI-shuhn)—computer software that can scan and analyze a person's face and match it to one stored in a database

logic (LOJ-ik)—careful and correct reasoning

milestone (MILE-stone)—an important event or development

program (PROH-gram)—a series of step-by-step instructions that tells a computer what to do

sensor (SEN-sur)—an instrument that detects changes in the environment and sends the information to a controlling device

supercomputer (SOO-pur-kuhm-pyoo-tur)—the fastest and most powerful computer available

technology (tek-NOL-uh-jee)—the use of science and engineering to do practical things and solve problems

trait (TRATE)—a quality or characteristic that makes one thing different from another

treatment (TREET-muhnt)—a process or medicine used to take care of someone who is sick

READ MORE

Jackson, Tom. *Artificial Intelligence.* London: Macmillan Children's Books, 2022.

Pattison, Darcy. *A.I.: How Patterns Helped Artificial Intelligence Defeat World Champion Lee Sedol.* Little Rock, AR: Mims House, 2021.

Williams, Dinah. *Artificial Intelligence.* New York: Starry Forest Books, Inc., 2021.

INTERNET SITES

Artificial Intelligence Facts for Kids
kids.kiddle.co/Artificial_intelligence

How Does the Machine Learn?
edsquare.co/ml/

National Geographic Kids: The Life of Alan Turing
natgeokids.com/uk/discover/history/general-history/the-life-of-alan-turing/

ABOUT THE AUTHOR

Carol Kim is the author of several fiction and nonfiction books for kids. She enjoys researching and uncovering little-known facts and sharing what she learns with young readers. Carol lives in Austin, Texas, with her family. Learn more about her and her latest books at her website, CarolKimBooks.com.

ABOUT THE ILLUSTRATOR

Erik Doescher is an illustrator that specializes in licensed art for publishing, style guides, and merchandising. He has worked in the industry for over 25 years, and his clients include DC Comics, Penguin/Random House, Nickelodeon, Golden Books, Hasbro, The Walt Disney Company, Capstone, and Warner Brothers.